GNU Octave by Example

A Fast and Practical Approach
to Learning GNU Octave

Ashwin Pajankar
Sharvani Chandu

Apress®

GNU Octave by Example: A Fast and Practical Approach to Learning GNU Octave

Ashwin Pajankar
Nashik, Maharashtra, India

Sharvani Chandu
Pittsburgh, PA, USA

ISBN-13 (pbk): 978-1-4842-6085-2
https://doi.org/10.1007/978-1-4842-6086-9

ISBN-13 (electronic): 978-1-4842-6086-9

Managing Director, Apress Media LLC: Welmoed Spahr
Acquisitions Editor: Aditee Mirashi
Development Editor: Matthew Moodie
Coordinating Editor: Shrikant Vishwakarma

Cover designed by eStudioCalamar

Cover image designed by Freepik (www.freepik.com)

Distributed to the book trade worldwide by Springer Science+Business Media New York, 233 Spring Street, 6th Floor, New York, NY 10013. Phone 1-800-SPRINGER, fax (201) 348-4505, e-mail orders-ny@springer-sbm.com, or visit www.springeronline.com. Apress Media, LLC is a California LLC and the sole member (owner) is Springer Science + Business Media Finance Inc (SSBM Finance Inc). SSBM Finance Inc is a **Delaware** corporation.

For information on translations, please e-mail booktranslations@springernature.com; for reprint, paperback, or audio rights, please e-mail bookpermissions@springernature.com.

Apress titles may be purchased in bulk for academic, corporate, or promotional use. eBook versions and licenses are also available for most titles. For more information, reference our Print and eBook Bulk Sales web page at www.apress.com/bulk-sales.

Any source code or other supplementary material referenced by the author in this book is available to readers on GitHub via the book's product page, located at www.apress.com/978-1-4842-6085-2. For more detailed information, please visit www.apress.com/source-code.

Printed on acid-free paper

I dedicate this book to
Srinivasa Ramanujan,
the great Indian Mathematician
—Ashwin Pajankar

My parents and my sisters who have been
my constant support
—Sharvani Chandu

Table of Contents

About the Authors

Ashwin Pajankar holds a Master of Technology from IIIT Hyderabad. He started programming and tinkering with electronics at the tender age of seven, beginning with the BASIC programming language. He was gradually exposed to C programming, 8085, and x86 assembly programming during his higher secondary schooling. He is proficient in x86 assembly, C, Java, Python, and shell programming. He is also proficient with Raspberry Pi, Arduino, and other single-board computers and microcontrollers. Ashwin is passionate about training and mentoring. He has trained more than 60,000 students and professionals in live and online training courses. He has published more than a dozen books with many international and Indian publishers. He has also reviewed numerous books and educational video courses. This is his fourth book with Apress and he is working on more books. He regularly conducts programming bootcamps and hands-on training for software companies. He is also an avid YouTuber with more than 10,000 subscribers to his channel. You can find him on LinkedIn.

Sharvani Chandu holds an MS in Computer Vision from CMU and a BTech in Electronics and Communication Engineering from IIIT Hyderabad. She has research experience in the areas of computer vision and machine learning. She currently works for Amazon; she also worked in Bangalore as a software engineer for a couple of years, focusing on machine learning and natural language processing. During her undergraduate and graduate studies, she worked as a research intern, teaching assistant, and research assistant. She has also published research papers related to her work. She is enthusiastic about working in the areas of mathematics, computer vision, and programming. You can find her on LinkedIn.

About the Technical Reviewer

 **Lentin Joseph** is an author, roboticist, and robotics entrepreneur from India. He runs a robotics software company called Qbotics Labs in Kochi/Kerala. He has 10 years of experience in the robotics domain primarily in Robot Operating System (ROS), OpenCV, and PCL. He has authored eight books on ROS, including *Learning Robotics Using Python*, first and second editions, *Mastering ROS for Robotics Programming*, first and second editions; *ROS Robotics Projects*, first and second editions; and *Robot Operating System for Absolute Beginners*. He pursued his Masters in Robotics and Automation from India and has worked at the Robotics Institute, CMU, USA. He is also a TEDx speaker.

Acknowledgments

We want to express our gratitude to the technical reviewer and long-time acquaintance, Lentin Joseph, for helping us make this book better. We would also like to express our gratitude to the team from Apress. Aditee Mirashi helped us coordinate the entire book process and Shrikant Vishwakarma guided us through the editorial process. We are thankful to Celestin Suresh for giving us the opportunity to write this book.

Introduction

During my days studying as an undergraduate student, I used MATLAB for demonstrations in the areas of image and signal processing. MATLAB is indeed a good tool and a very convenient programming interface for people who want to focus on subject matters like image and signal processing because it provides excellent support in these areas for demonstrations. However, MATLAB is a paid and non-open source product.

GNU Octave is an open source alternative to MATLAB. It has a very high degree of compatibility with MATLAB in terms of programming. One of the most desired features of GNU Octave is that it can be used with Jupyter Notebook. This makes it easier for everyone to write interactive scripts and share them.

The GNU Octave project has an online repository called the Octaveforge that hosts many useful libraries for tasks in the areas of signal and image processing. You can create publication-quality visualizations for scientific datasets using GNU Octave.

We wrote this book in such a way that novices and beginners will find it easy to learn the important concepts. The step-by-step approach gradually increases in rigor and difficulty of concepts and demonstrations. People working in the areas of data science, signal and image processing, and scientific domains will find this book extremely useful to get introduced to GNU Octave and Jupyter Notebook.

While this book has been written for novices and beginners, it is recommended that you have had some exposure to computer programming and mathematics since a lot of the concepts in this book are related to mathematics.

We hope that this book serves you, the reader, well and that you will enjoy this book as much as we enjoyed writing it.

CHAPTER 1

Introduction to GNU Octave

We hope you have gone through the table of contents and the preface. If not, we highly recommend you do so. This is the very first chapter of this book and we welcome you to the exciting journey of learning GNU Octave.

In this chapter, you will learn the details of GNU Octave such as its history, applications, limitations, and a comparison with other contemporary and similar tools. This chapter is mostly dedicated to general information about GNU Octave and its installation on various popular OS platforms such as Windows, Ubuntu, and Raspberry Pi Raspbian. You will not be writing any programs or learning about the functionality of GNU Octave here. The following is the list of topics you will learn about in this chapter:

- The GNU Octave Project

- Applications

- Limitations

- The community

- Comparison with other tools

- Installation of GNU Octave on various platforms

- Working with GNU Octave in different modes

© Ashwin Pajankar and Sharvani Chandu 2020
A. Pajankar and S. Chandu, *GNU Octave by Example*,
https://doi.org/10.1007/978-1-4842-6086-9_1

The GNU Octave Project

GNU Octave is a high-level programming language. It is used for numerical and scientific computing. It is part of the GNU Project so it is free and open-source. In fact, anyone with the necessary skill set and will to so can contribute to its development. The homepage of GNU Octave is located at www.gnu.org/software/octave. It is basically a mathematics-oriented programming language with convenient and easy-to-learn visualization tools for scientific researchers.

The Octave interpreter is written in the C++ programming language. Octave is an interpreted programming language because it uses the Octave interpreter to run the Octave scripting language statements and scripts. Octave has a lot of dynamically loadable modules. Octave uses OpenGL or gnuplot for plotting. Octave has both a GUI (graphical user interface) and a CLI (command line interface). If any of you have experience with working with an OS shell interpreter or the Python programming language, consider Octave as almost the same as working with shell or Python programming.

History of the GNU Octave Project

The GNU Octave Project started in 1988 as a companion for a textbook that was under development for chemical engineering undergraduate students. This was done after the faculty members observed that chemical engineering students were spending a lot of time debugging FORTRAN issues, which was used for their programming exercises. Full-time development began in 1992. Gradually it became a part of the GNU Project. The following is a timeline that shows the major milestones in the development of GNU Octave:

- 1988: Conception of idea

- 1992: Beginning of full-time development

- 1994: Version 1.x.x

- 1996: Version 2.0.x and Windows port

- 2007: Version 4.0

- 2015: Version 4.0.0 with stable GUI

- 2019: Octave 5.1.0

Applications of Octave

Octave is used to solve different scientific and numerical computational problems. It can be used for linear programming and optimization. Octave is also deployed on many supercomputers because it supports parallel programming. You can find GNU Octave deployed at supercomputers in the Ohio Supercomputer Center (`www.osc.edu/resources/available_ software/software_list/octave`), the Oak Ridge National Laboratory (`www.olcf.ornl.gov/software_package/octave`), the and University of Minnesota (`www.msi.umn.edu/sw/octave`). In the research community, Octave is actively used for data analytics, image processing, computer vision, economic research, data mining, statistical analysis, machine learning, signal processing, and many more scientific applications. You will learn how to demonstrate programs pertaining to a lot of the above-mentioned scientific computing areas with GNU Octave.

Limitations and Drawbacks of Octave

The Octave programming language was primarily developed to perform numerical and scientific computations. It is not supposed to be used as a general purpose programming language like C and C++. Also, it is our opinion that you should always choose a programming language suitable for your own programming or computational needs. If you are looking to do some system-level programming, then C and assembly languages are your friend. However, if you are a subject matter expert (for example, a chemical engineer or a signal processing professional) who cannot spare enough time to learn the intricacies of a programming language like C, then you should use GNU Octave or the Python programming language because you can quickly write code snippets to prototype your ideas.

We mentioned that GNU Octave is an interpreted programming language. This means that it first converts the code or statements into a machine-readable code format before the computer executes them. The main drawback is that the program executes slowly compared to programs written in compiled languages such as C or Fortran. And it is certainly slower than assembly. The main advantage of this approach is that the statements are easy to write and change, and the programmer does not have to compile the code before executing it. It gives a very high degree of control to the programmers. This is why Octave is not the first choice when it comes to system programming or fast or parallel programs on a supercomputer. The C programming language is more suitable for such applications. However, as you will experience later in the book, Octave lets you solve very advanced and computationally demanding problems with only a few instructions or commands and with satisfactory speed.

Comparison of Octave with Alternatives

Octave is a part of GNU, thus it is a free and open-source package and programming environment for numerical and scientific computations. Many times it is promoted as a free alternative for MATLAB. MATLAB is a short form of Matrix Laboratory. It is also a programming environment and language for numerical and scientific computing. MATLAB is developed and maintained by Mathworks. It is a proprietary and commercial software. Octave tries to maintain a very high degree of syntax compatibility with MATLAB. Many of the programs we will demonstrate can be directly run as they are with MATLAB. Keep in mind that this applies to many, but not all, of the programs.

The other free alternatives of MATLAB are Scilab and FreeMat. The Scilab project does not attempt much to maintain syntax-level compatibility with MATLAB and Octave. The FreeMat project has not been updated since 2013.

The Online Octave Community

You can find all of the information and downloadable setup files for Octave at the project website at `www.octave.org`. Here you'll find the official manual, a Wiki page with tricks and tips (`https://wiki.octave.org/GNU_Octave_Wiki`), latest news, a more detailed history, and other relevant information. You can also get involved in the development; visit `www.gnu.org/software/octave/get-involved.html` for more information. StackOverflow is a good source of information and help. You can find questions related to Octave at `https://stackoverflow.com/questions/tagged/octave`.

There many additional packages that do not come preinstalled with the standard Octave distribution. Many of them can be downloaded from Octave Forge at `https://octave.sourceforge.io`. Octave Forge is a community project for collaborative development of GNU Octave extensions, called Octave packages. Here you can find specially designed packages for scientific and numerical applications such as image processing, signal processing, economics, information theory, analytical mathematics, and so on.

Installing GNU Octave

In this section, you will learn how to install GNU Octave on multiple platforms such as Windows, Ubuntu, and Raspberry Pi. All of the code examples and interactive sessions we demonstrate in this book have been tested on these platforms by the authors. So, let's begin.

Installing on Windows

You can install GNU Octave on Windows by downloading and executing the installable file from the Octave download page at www.gnu.org/software/octave/download.html. This page has options for 32-bit and 64-bit computers. There is an option for **linear algebra for large data** but you will not need it for this book. So, choose the .exe file for installing to 32-bit or 64-bit Windows computers. Other formats, 7z and .zip, are also available. But you should go for the .exe file. Download the file and execute it to install GNU Octave. Once the setup has completed successfully, add the directory location of the Octave executable to the Windows PATH variable. In my case, it is C:\Octave\Octave-5.2.0\mingw64\bin. It could be different for you based on the GNU Octave version and your computer architecture (32-bit or 64-bit).

Once you are done installing it, you need to install Python 3 because you will need the pip3 utility of Python 3 to install Jupyter Notebook and Octave Kernel for it. Also, in the end, you will learn how to connect Python 3 with GNU. You will use the Python 3 interpreter at that time. Visit the Python 3 download page located at www.python.org/downloads/ and download the setup file of Python 3 for your computer, as shown in Figure 1-1.

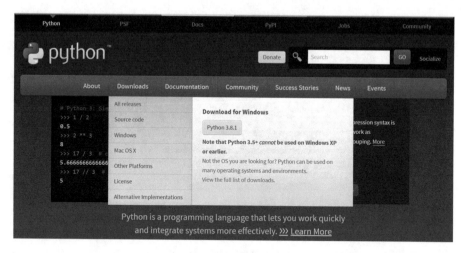

Figure 1-1. *Python project homepage*

Run the setup file to install Python 3. During installation, check the checkbox related to adding Python 3 to the PATH variable, as shown in Figure 1-2.

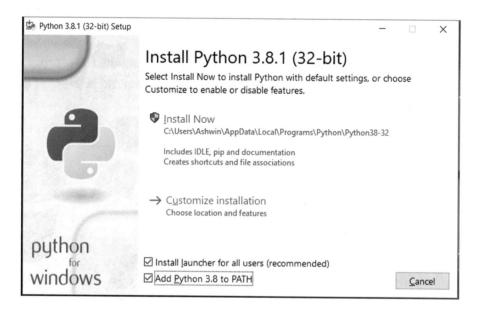

Figure 1-2. *Python Installation Wizard*

Also, choose the **Customize installation** option. This will show you more options, as shown in Figure 1-3.

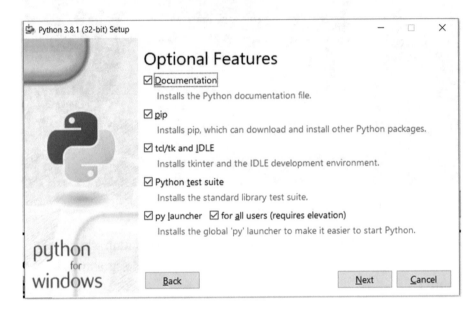

Figure 1-3. *Python installation options*

Check all the boxes and click the **Next** button to continue the setup. Complete the setup. Once done, run the following command at the Windows command prompt **cmd**:

```
python -V
```

It will return the version of Python 3 as follows:

```
Python 3.8.1
```

You can also check the version of **pip3** as follows:

```
pip3 -V
```

pip stands for **Pip installs Python** or **Pip installs Packages**. Its name is a recursive acronym. It is a package manager for the Python programming language. You can install the other needed components for our demonstrations with pip. To install **Jupyter**, run the following command at the command prompt:

```
pip3 install jupyter
```

Jupyter is an interactive environment for various programming language. You will see the details of Jupyter at the end of this chapter.

To install the Octave Kernel for Jupyter, run the following command:

```
pip3 install octave_kernel
```

The Octave Kernel for Jupyter allows us to run the Octave programs in a Jupyter notebook. As mentioned, you will see how to work with GNU Octave and Jupyter in the end of this chapter.

Installation on Ubuntu Linux

Ubuntu Linux is a distribution based on Debian Linux. Both are popular Linux distributions. Python 3 and pip3 come preinstalled in Ubuntu so you do not have to install them separately. First, update the package list for upgrades by running the following command in the **terminal** program:

```
sudo apt-get update
```

Then install GNU Octave with the following command:

```
sudo apt install octave -y
```

Then using **pip3**, install Jupyter and the Octave Kernel as follows:

```
pip3 install jupyter
pip3 install octave_kernel
```

Run the above commands and complete the setup.

Installation on Raspberry Pi with Raspbian OS

Raspberry Pi is a popular single board computer. If a desktop computer or a laptop is out of your budget, you can opt for a Raspberry Pi. The recommended operating system for Raspberry Pi is Raspbian OS, which is a Debian derivative for the ARM processor architecture that Raspberry Pi boards use. The setup of Raspberry Pi is outside of the scope of this book, but you can find detailed instructions at www.raspberrypi.org. Once you get your Raspberry Pi ready, you can run the following commands on the **lxterminal**, which is the terminal emulator for Raspbian OS, so to install Octave, Jupyter Notebook, and Jupyter Kernel, type these commands:

```
sudo apt-get update
sudo apt-get install octave -y
sudo pip3 uninstall ipykernel
sudo pip3 install ipykernel==4.8.0
sudo pip3 install jupyter
sudo pip3 install prompt-toolkit==2.0.5
sudo pip3 install octave_kernel
```

Running the above commands in sequence will install all of the required packages for this demonstration on the Raspbian OS of Raspberry Pi.

Exploring GNU Octave

Let's start exploring various aspects of GNU Octave. We will start with GUI.

Octave GUI

When you install Octave on Windows, you also get a shortcut to the Octave GUI on your desktop. There is another way to launch it. You can search for it in the search box of Windows by typing **Octave**. Two options will appear:

Octave GUI and **Octave CLI**. Choose the GUI option. On Ubuntu, you can launch it by searching for it in the search box and clicking the Octave icon displayed in the search output, as shown in Figure 1-4.

Figure 1-4. *GNU Octave on Ubuntu*

In the Raspberry Pi Raspbian OS menu (the raspberry fruit icon located at the top left corner on the Raspbian OS desktop), you can find it under Education, as shown in Figure 1-5.

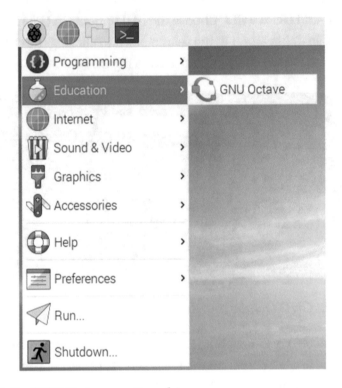

Figure 1-5. *GNU Octave on Raspbian*

When you launch GNU Octave the very first time on the Raspberry Pi with Raspbian OS, it shows the welcome message window, as shown in Figure 1-6.

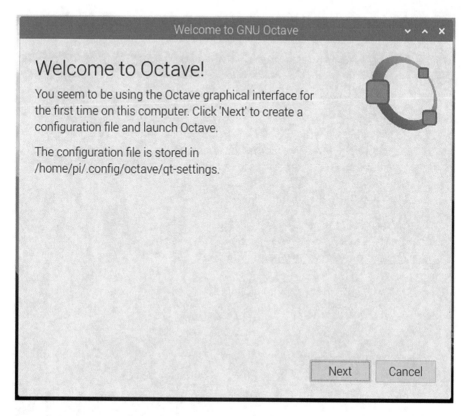

Figure 1-6. *GNU Octave welcome screen*

Click the **Next** button and you will see the window shown in Figure 1-7.

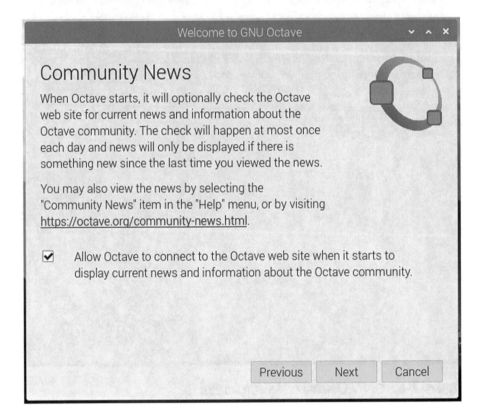

Figure 1-7. *Community news*

It is recommended to check the checkbox (to receive latest news and information about the Octave community). Click the **Next** button and you'll see the window shown in Figure 1-8.

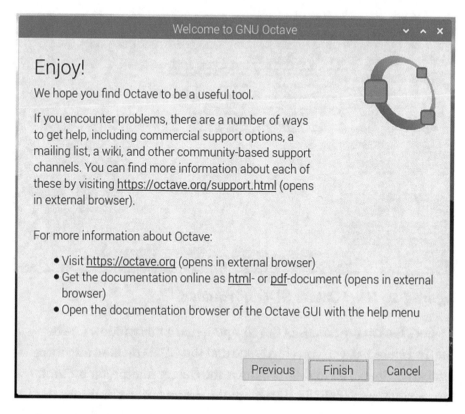

Figure 1-8. *Help information*

Click the **Finish** button and the Octave GUI will be launched.

The GUI Window looks the same on all platforms. Figure 1-9 shows the Octave GUI window running on a Windows computer.

Figure 1-9. *GNU Octave GUI on Windows*

Let's look at the details of the components in this window one by one. In Figure 1-9, you can clearly see that the GUI is divided into three vertical sections. The middle section is the Octave interpreter prompt. You can interact with it like the command prompt of an OS. It runs the Octave statements, which you will see soon. The vertical section on the right is the **variable editor**. The vertical section on the left is divided into three sub-sections: a **file browser**, a **workspace**, and a **command history** window. You can rearrange these spaces anytime you want by dragging and dropping them within the GUI window.

The top offers a menubar with the usual file operations and their shortcuts. And if you pay close attention, in the bottom of the window, you'll see three tabs that read **Command Window**, **Editor**, and **Documentation**. The command window is the interactive mode command prompt that you can see in the screenshot. The Editor tab opens a code editor window, and Documentation will bring up an index of the browsable documentation. You will explore all of these things one by one.

But first, let's get started with the customary **Hello World!** program. Go to the interactive window and type in `printf("Hello, World!\n");` and then press Enter. It prints the string enclosed in the double quotes in the interactive window, as shown in Figure 1-10.

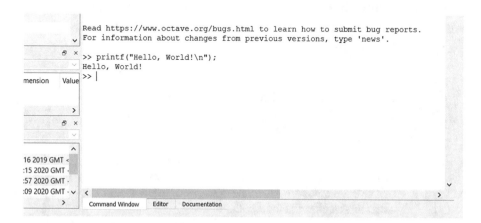

Figure 1-10. *The command window of the GNU Octave GUI*

You can even create a single-line program of this code and save it. Go to the editor by choosing the Editor tab at the bottom. Type the same line as above in the editor and save it. Octave automatically assigns the `.m` extension to the file. MATLAB uses the same extension. The simple program is shown in Figure 1-11.

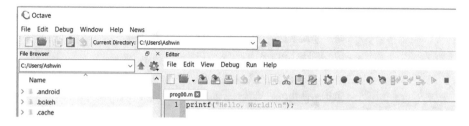

Figure 1-11. *A simple program*

Here, we saved the program on the disk in the computer. Under the Editor section, you can see all the options any IDE (integrated development environment) has. You can change the font in the editor by pressing the ***Ctrl*** key on the keyboard and moving the scroll wheel of the mouse at the same time. After saving, click the Run symbol (the gear and yellow triangle; in Linux, it is a paper plane). After that, it shows the dialog box, as shown in Figure 1-12.

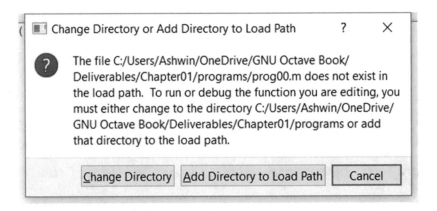

Figure 1-12. *Dialog box to load path*

Click the **Add Directory to the Load Path** button. The program is executed by the Octave interpreter and you can see the output in the interactive tab, as shown in Figure 1-13.

```
>> printf("Hello, World!\n");
Hello, World!
>>

>> prog00

Hello, World!
```

Figure 1-13. *Output of the simple program*

As you can see, it prints the program name without the extension and then shows the output.

Congratulations! You have just run your first GNU Octave program.

Octave CLI

You can also launch the command line independently. In Windows, you can either search for Octave and choose **Octave CLI** from the results or you can run the command octave in the command prompt to launch the CLI. In the Linux flavors like Ubuntu and Raspbian OS, you can run the same command, octave, in the command prompt to launch the Octave CLI. In order to exit the CLI, you must run the exit command. You can also run the .m octave files from the command prompt using the Octave interpreter. Suppose, on Windows, that the absolute path of your Octave program file is C:\Book\Chapter01\programs\prog00.m. You can execute the program using the Octave interpreter by running the following command at the command prompt:

```
octave "C:\Book\Chapter01\programs\prog00.m"
```

Similarly, on Raspberry Pi, suppose the absolute path of the Octave program file is /home/pi/prog00.m. You can run it from the command prompt with the following command:

```
octave "/home/pi/prog00.m"
```

Octave Programming with Jupyter Notebook

Jupyter Notebook is web-based notebook that is used for interactive programming of various programming languages like Python, Octave, Julia, and R. It is very popular with people who work in research domains. A Jupyter notebook can have code, visualizations, output, and rich text.

The advantage of a Jupyter notebook over Octave's own interactive prompt is that you can edit the code and see the new output instantly, which is not possible in the Octave command prompt. Another advantage is that you have the code and output in the same document. You can even share it on the cloud. There are many services online that help you store and execute your Jupyter notebook scripts on cloud servers.

Let's see how to use Jupyter Notebook for writing and executing Octave code. Open the command prompt of your OS (cmd in Windows, terminal in Ubuntu, and lxterminal in Raspbian OS). Run the following command there:

```
jupyter notebook
```

The Jupyter Notebook server process will be launched and the command prompt window will show a server log, as shown in Figure 1-14.

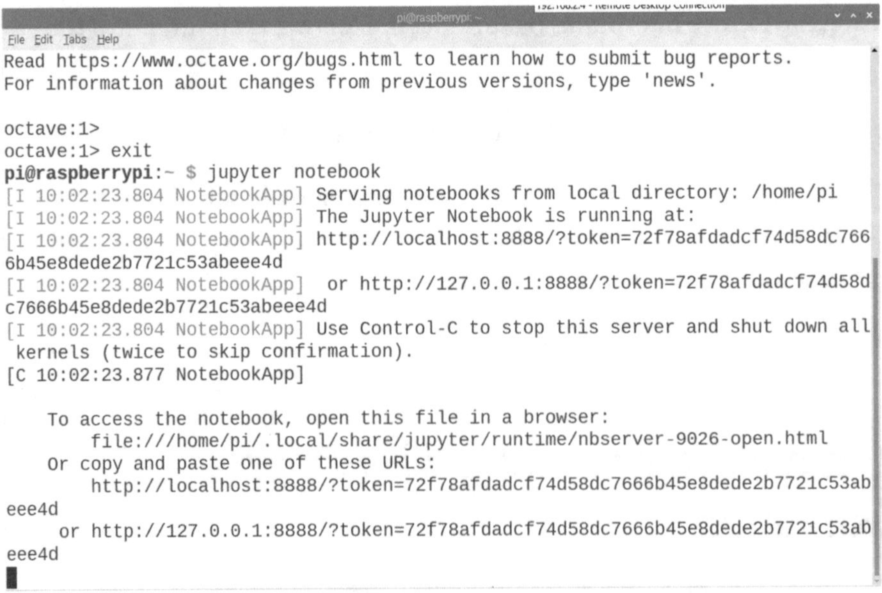

Figure 1-14. Launching a new Jupyter Notebook process

Also, it launches a webpage in the default browser in the OS. If the browser window is already open, it launches the page in a new tab of the same browser window. Another way to open the page (in case you accidentally close this browser window) is to visit `http://localhost:8888/` in your browser. Figure 1-15 shows the page you'll see.

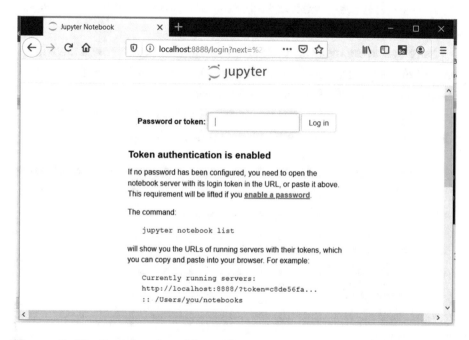

Figure 1-15. *Logging in with a token*

The token can be found in the server logs. The following is a sample server log with tokens. To access the notebook, open this file in a browser:

```
file:///C:/Users/Ashwin/AppData/Roaming/jupyter/
runtime/nbserver-8420-open.html
Alternatively, you can copy and paste one of these URLs:
    http://localhost:8888/?token=e4a4fab0d8c22cd01b6530d5da
    ced19d32d7e0c3a56f925c
 or http://127.0.0.1:8888/?token=e4a4fab0d8c22cd01b6530d5da
ced19d32d7e0c3a56f925c
```

In the log above, you can see a couple of URLs. They refer to the same page (localhost and 127.0.0.1 are the same hosts). You can either directly copy and paste any of these URLs into the address bar of the browser tab and open the Jupyter Notebook homepage or you can visit `http://localhost:8888/` as discussed and then paste the token in the server log (in this case, it is `e4a4fab0d8c22cd01b6530d5daced19d32d7e0c3a56f925c`) and log in. It will take you to the same homepage.

Note that every instance of the Jupyter Notebook server will have its own token, and the token here will not work with your Jupyter Notebook. The token is only valid for that server process.

So, if you follow any one of the routes explained above, you will see a homepage tab in the browser window, as shown in Figure 1-16.

Figure 1-16. *A new homepage tab of Jupyter Notebook*

As you can see, there are three tabs in the webpage itself: **Files**, **Running**, and **Clusters**. The Files tab shows the directories and files in the directory from where you launched the notebook server from the command prompt. In the above example, we executed the command `jupyter notebook` from **lxterminal** of our Raspberry Pi. And the present working directory is the ***home*** directory of the ***pi*** user /home/pi. This is why we can see all the files and directories in the home directory of our RPi computer in Figure 1-16.

In the top right corner are the **Quit** and **Logout** buttons. If you click the Logout button, it logs out from the current session; in order to log in, you need the token or URL with the embedded token from the notebook server log, as discussed. If you click the Quit button, it stops the notebook server process running in the command prompt and shows the modal message box, as shown in Figure 1-17.

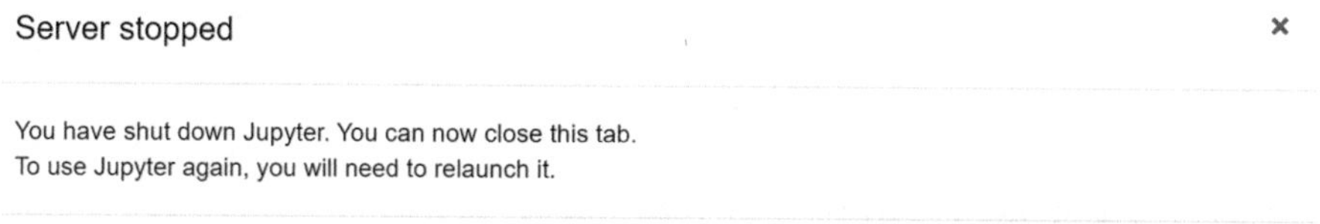

Server stopped   ✕

You have shut down Jupyter. You can now close this tab.
To use Jupyter again, you will need to relaunch it.

Figure 1-17. *The message shown after clicking the Quit button*

In order to work with it again, you need to execute the command jupyter notebook again in the command prompt.

On the top right side, just below the Quit and Logout buttons is a small button with the refresh symbol. It is the refresh button. It refreshes the homepage. You can also see the **New** button. Once clicked, it shows a dropdown menu, as shown in Figure 1-18.

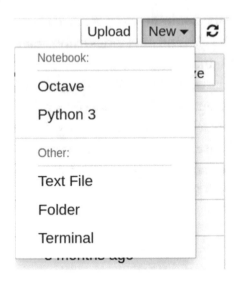

Figure 1-18. *Options for a new notebook*

As you can see, the dropdown is divided into two sections: **Notebook** and **Other**. You can create Octave and Python 3 notebooks. If your computer has other languages installed that are supported by Jupyter notebook, those languages will show up here. You can also create text files and folders. You can open the command prompt in the web browser by clicking **Terminal**. The output of **lxterminal** running in a separate web browser tab is shown in Figure 1-19.

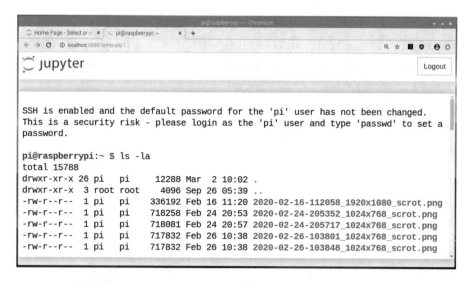

Figure 1-19. *A new lxterminal window within the browser*

Clicking Octave in the dropdown creates a new Octave notebook, as shown in Figure 1-20.

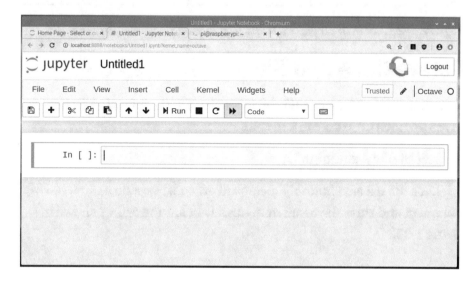

Figure 1-20. *A new GNU Octave notebook*

If you go to the homepage again by clicking the homepage tab in the browser and then opening the **Running** tab in the homepage, you can see the entries corresponding to the terminal and the Octave notebook, as shown in Figure 1-21.

Figure 1-21. *Summary of current Jupyter Notebook subprocesses*

Octave Code and Richtext in Notebook

Go to the Octave **Untitled1** tab again and type in the following statement in the text area (also known as a cell):

```
printf("Hello, World!\n");
```

Click the Execute button. Jupyter will execute the code as an Octave statement and show the result immediately below the cell, as shown in Figure 1-22.

Figure 1-22. *Code output in Jupyter Notebook*

As you can see, after execution, it automatically creates a new cell below the result and sets the cursor there. Let's discuss the menu bar and the icons above the programming cells. You can save the file by clicking the floppy disc icon. You can add a new empty cell after the current cell by clicking the + icon. The next three icons are for cutting, copying, and pasting. The up and down arrows can shift the position of the current cell up and down, respectively. The next option is to run the cell, which you already saw in action. The next three icons are to interrupt the kernel, restart the kernel, and restart the kernel and rerun all the cells in the notebook. Next is a dropdown menu that tells you what type of cell it should be. Figure 1-23 shows the options when the dropdown menu is clicked.

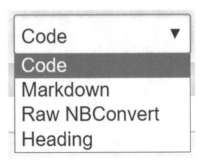

Figure 1-23. *Types of cells in a Jupyter notebook*

The cell is treated as an Octave code cell when you choose the **Code** option. It is treated as a Markdown cell when you choose the **Markdown** option. Markdown is a markup language that can create rich text output. For example, anything followed by # creates a heading, anything followed by ## creates a sub-heading, and so on. Just type the following lines in a markdown cell and execute them:

```
# Heading 1
## Heading 2
```

During our Octave demonstrations, we will mostly use markdown for headings. However, you can further explore markdown on your own. You can find more information about it at `https://jupyter-notebook.readthedocs.io/en/stable/examples/Notebook/Working%20With%20Markdown%20Cells.html`. The output of the demonstration above is shown in Figure 1-24.

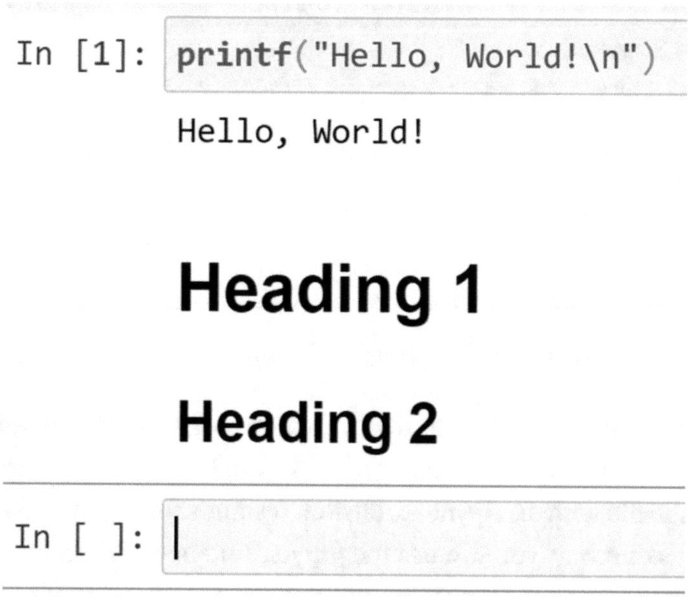

```
In [1]:  printf("Hello, World!\n")

         Hello, World!
```

Heading 1

Heading 2

```
In [ ]:  |
```

Figure 1-24. *Headings in Markdown mode*

You can even change the name of the notebook file by clicking its name in the top part of the notebook. You'll see a modal box for renaming it, as shown in Figure 1-25.

Rename Notebook   ×

Enter a new notebook name:

Untitled1

Cancel   Rename

Figure 1-25. *Renaming a notebook in Jupyter*

Rename it if you wish to do so. If you browse the location on disc from where you launched the Jupyter notebook from the command prompt, you will find the file with an .ipynb extension. It stands for **IPython Notebook**.

In the same way, you can use the Jupyter notebook for doing interactive programming with the other programming languages that support Jupyter. You will mostly use this notebook format to store your code snippets for interactive sessions. This is because everything is saved in a single file, which can be shared easily, as discussed. You will also see how to add code to .m files and execute it to see the visual output as you proceed further in this book.

You can clear the output of a cell or the entire notebook. In the menu bar, click the **Cell** menu. In the dropdown, **Current Outputs** and **All Output** have a **Clear** option, which clears the output of the cells. The options are shown in Figure 1-26.

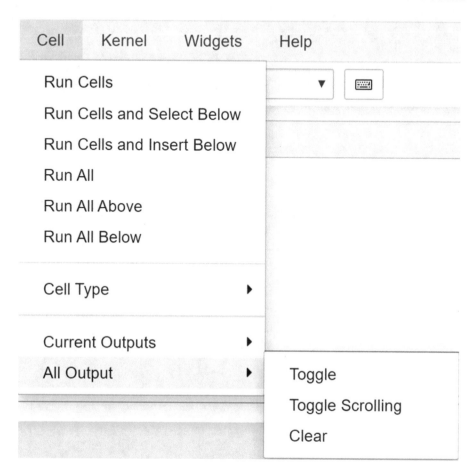

Figure 1-26. *Clearing output in Jupyter*

Summary

In this chapter, you got started with Octave installation on various platforms. You then explored how to run a simple statement in various ways. You also studied Jupyter Notebook and its use in scientific and numerical programming with Octave. This chapter was a bit light on the programming part. However, from the next chapter onwards, you will dive deeper into programming with GNU Octave.

CHAPTER 2

Getting Started with GNU Octave and Jupyter

In Chapter 1, you learned in detail how to get your Windows computer, Linux, and Raspberry Pi ready for working with GNU Octave and Jupyter Notebook. You also learned how to get started with GNU Octave programming and Jupyter Notebook. In this chapter, you will delve deeper into GNU Octave programming and you will mostly use Jupyter Notebook for programming demonstrations in interactive mode. The following is the list of topics you will learn and demonstrate in this chapter:

- Simple mathematical operations

- Built-in mathematical constants

- Getting help

- Variables in GNU Octave

- Global variables

- Conventions for naming variables

- Clearing the command prompt

© Ashwin Pajankar and Sharvani Chandu 2020
A. Pajankar and S. Chandu, *GNU Octave by Example*,
https://doi.org/10.1007/978-1-4842-6086-9_2

Simple Mathematical Operations

Let's get started with some simple concepts. In this section, you will learn how to perform simple mathematical operations on numerical operands. It is recommended to create a new notebook for every chapter and save all of the notebooks in the same directory on your computer. So create a new notebook and create a markup cell with a heading that says **Simple Mathematical Operations**. Then run the following statement in the next cell:

```
2 + 5
```

It will execute and show the following output:

```
ans =   7
```

Similarly, run the following statements and see the output:

```
2 - 5
5 / 2
2 / 5
5 % 2
5 * 2
2 ^ 5
```

After executing the statements above, you'll get the output shown in Figure 2-1.

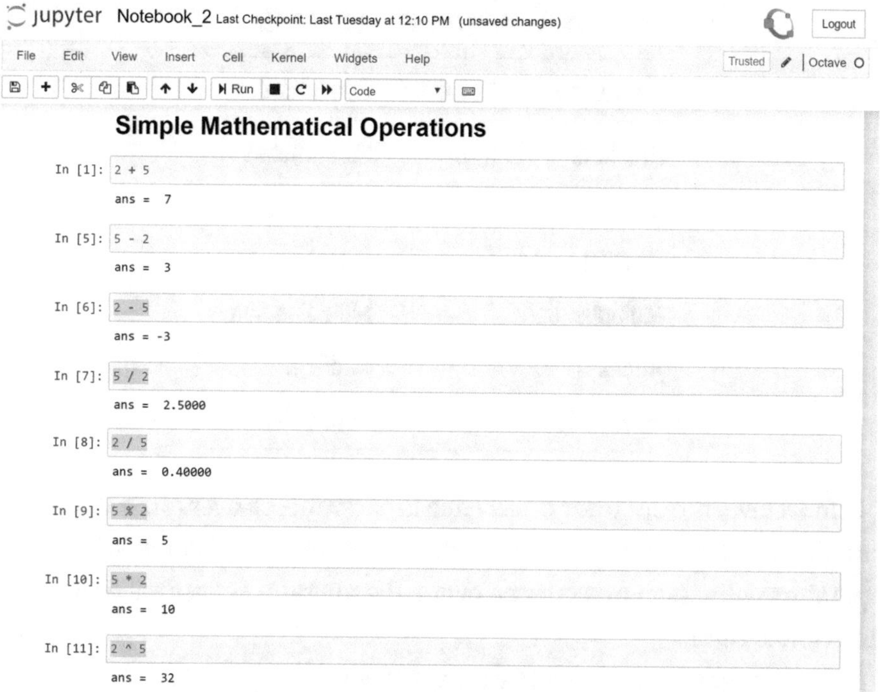

Figure 2-1. *Screenshot of the simple mathematical operations in action*

When various operators are used in a single expression, the operator precedence is similar to the behavior you find in mathematics or other programming languages. In mathematics, it is commonly referred to as BODMAS or PEDMAS, which is shown in Table 2-1.

Table 2-1. BODMAS/PEDMAS

Operation	Notation	Operation
Brackets	{[( )]}	**P**arentheses
Orders	^, **	**E**xponents
Division	/	**D**ivision
Multiplication	*	**M**ultiplication
Addition	+	**A**ddition
Subtraction	-	**S**ubtraction

In Octave, the operator preference is parentheses over other operators, and division and multiplication over addition and subtraction. When operators with equal precedence occur, the operator precedence goes from left to right.

For example, the answer to the expression

```
10 * 5 - (5 + 2)^2 + 10 / 5
```

```
10 * 5 - 7^2 + 10 / 5
expression inside the parentheses is computed
10 * 5 - 49 + 10 / 5
exponents are computed
50 - 49 + 2
division and multiplication (operators of equal precedence) are
computed
3
addition and subtraction (operators of equal precedence) are
computed
```

You can run this complex expression in a new cell. It will execute the following output:

```
ans = 3
```

It is advisable to use parentheses when writing complex expressions because they overrule any operator, make your code readable, and you can avoid mistakes that are easy to overlook.

Built-in Mathematical Constants

There are many built-in mathematical constants in GNU Octave. In a new cell, create a markdown cell with a heading that says **Built-in Mathematical Constants**. You can retrieve them in multiple formats. Run the following code:

```
e
```

This returns the value of the constant e that is the base of natural logarithms:

```
ans =  2.7183
```

Run the following code:

```
e(3)
```

It returns a 3x3 matrix of es as follows:

```
ans =

   2.7183   2.7183   2.7183
   2.7183   2.7183   2.7183
   2.7183   2.7183   2.7183
```

You will learn about matrices in the next chapter. You can even have a custom sized matrix of es as follows:

```
e(3, 2)
ans =
   2.7183   2.7183
   2.7183   2.7183
   2.7183   2.7183
```

You can also create a matrix of more than two dimensions:

```
e(2, 2, 3)
ans =
ans(:,:,1) =
   2.7183    2.7183
   2.7183    2.7183
ans(:,:,2) =
   2.7183    2.7183
   2.7183    2.7183
ans(:,:,3) =
   2.7183    2.7183
   2.7183    2.7183
```

You can have these constants in single (32-bit representation) or double (64-bit representation) precision as follows:

```
e(3, 2, class="single")
e(3, 2, class="double")
```

Similarly, there are other constants that can return a single value or matrices as demonstrated above. Let's look at each of them one by one. If you run pi, it returns the value of the constant pi. The constants i, j, I, and J return the imaginary unit that is $\sqrt{-1}$. Inf returns infinity and NaN returns **Not a Number**. The next three constants are system-dependent (processor-dependent, to be precise). The first one is eps. It returns the relative spacing between any two adjacent numbers in the machine's floating-point system representation. realmax returns the largest floating-point number, and realmin returns the smallest floating-point number represented by the system. Check these constants and their respective matrices yourself, like you did in the demonstration for the constant e.

Getting Help

You can get help for built-in constants and functions (you will learn about them later in the book). Suppose you want to get more information about the built-in constant pi. You can run the following in the command prompt of the GNU Octave GUI:

```
help pi
```

The output is shown in Figure 2-2.

```
>> help pi
'pi' is a built-in function from the file libinterp/corefcn/data.cc

 -- pi
 -- pi (N)
 -- pi (N, M)
 -- pi (N, M, K, ...)
 -- pi (..., CLASS)
     Return a scalar, matrix, or N-dimensional array whose elements are
     all equal to the ratio of the circumference of a circle to its
     diameter.

     Internally, 'pi' is computed as '4.0 * atan (1.0)'.

     When called with no arguments, return a scalar with the value of
     pi.

     When called with a single argument, return a square matrix with the
     dimension specified.

     When called with more than one scalar argument the first two
     arguments are taken as the number of rows and columns and any
     further arguments specify additional matrix dimensions.

     The optional argument CLASS specifies the return type and may be
     either "double" or "single".

     See also: e, I.

Additional help for built-in functions and operators is
available in the online version of the manual.  Use the command
'doc <topic>' to search the manual index.

Help and information about Octave is also available on the WWW
at https://www.octave.org and via the help@octave.org
mailing list.
>>
```

Figure 2-2. *The output of the command help*

Similarly, you can execute the following command for documentation:

```
doc pi
```

It opens the relevant documentation in the documentation tab of the GNU Octave GUI, as shown in Figure 2-3.

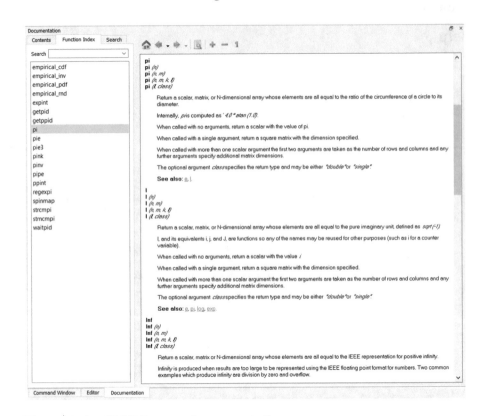

Figure 2-3. *GNU Octave documentation*

This way, you can find out more information about the built-in functions and constants offered by GNU Octave.

Variables in GNU Octave

A variable is an addressable memory (RAM) location where you can store data temporarily as long as your program (in script mode) or session (in interactive mode) is running. You can address the variable with a name. Each variable in the same program or session has a unique name. Let's look at how you can create a variable. Type and run the following statement:

```
a = 3.14
```

It will immediately show the value of variable a in the following line. = assigns the value on the left to the variable on the right (in the above case, a). You can suppress the display of output by adding ; to the statement as follows:

```
a = 3.14;
```

If you type the variable again in a new cell and execute it, it shows the value of the variable. You can also assign values to multiple variables as follows:

```
a = 1, b = 2, c = 3
a =   1
b =   2
c =   3
```

As you can see, you use the comma (,) between assign statements to do this.

We will discuss different types of variables later in this book.

Global Variables

There is a special way of declaring some variables as global variables: you use the keyword global before the variable name. The global variables may only be initialized once. If you run the following two lines one after the other

```
global a = 1
global a = 2
```

the variable a still contains a value of 1.

Using global variables has other benefits which will be addressed in later chapters.

Conventions for Naming Variables

In order to avoid errors and confusion while programming, you should adhere to the following conventions when naming variables:

- Names should not start with a number but you can use numbers in the variable name anywhere after the first character.

- Variable names are case sensitive.

- Names can include the underscore character.

- Keywords cannot be used as names of variables.

It is a good practice to use meaningful variable names because the code will be easier to read and debug.

You can retrieve the list of the current keywords in the Octave version by running the statement iskeyword(). The following is the list of reserved keywords in the current version of Octave:

```
ans =
{
  [1,1] = __FILE__
  [2,1] = __LINE__
  [3,1] = break
  [4,1] = case
  [5,1] = catch
  [6,1] = classdef
  [7,1] = continue
  [8,1] = do
  [9,1] = else
  [10,1] = elseif
  [11,1] = end
  [12,1] = end_try_catch
  [13,1] = end_unwind_protect
  [14,1] = endclassdef
  [15,1] = endenumeration
  [16,1] = endevents
  [17,1] = endfor
  [18,1] = endfunction
  [19,1] = endif
  [20,1] = endmethods
  [21,1] = endparfor
  [22,1] = endproperties
  [23,1] = endswitch
  [24,1] = endwhile
  [25,1] = enumeration
  [26,1] = events
  [27,1] = for
  [28,1] = function
  [29,1] = global
  [30,1] = if
  [31,1] = methods
```

```
   [32,1] = otherwise
   [33,1] = parfor
   [34,1] = persistent
   [35,1] = properties
   [36,1] = return
   [37,1] = switch
   [38,1] = try
   [39,1] = until
   [40,1] = unwind_protect
   [41,1] = unwind_protect_cleanup
   [42,1] = while
}
```

The commands who and whos show the list of variables and details, respectively. Create a few variables in Octave's interactive prompt in the GUI and run the command. First, create a few variables as follows:

```
>> a = 1;
>> b = 2;
>> c = 3;
```

The output of the who and whos commands and the workspace panel in the Octave GUI is shown in Figure 2-4.

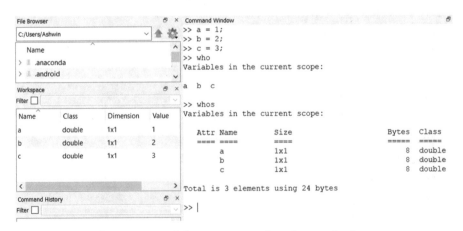

Figure 2-4. *The output of the commands who and whos*

Try running the commands who and whos in the Jupyter notebook too. The output will be the same. Many times, it is recommended to purge all the unused variables from memory. You are required to manage the memory manually when you handle large datasets. You can purge all the variables from memory with the command clear. If you run this command in the Octave GUI's command prompt, you can see all of the variables disappear from the workspace. Use the doc and help commands to obtain more information about the usage of clear.

Clearing the Command Prompt

You can clear the command prompt of Octave (running in terminal or the GUI, both) by running the clc command. You don't need to use this command in Jupyter Notebook. We discussed the methods to clear the output in the cells of Jupyter Notebook in the last chapter.

Summary

In this chapter, you learned about the basics of GNU Octave programming and explored the GUI interface in a bit more detail. The concepts you use in this book will be helpful to you in further chapters.

In the next chapter, you will explore different data types in GNU Octave in detail. The next chapter will be more coding-extensive than this one.

CHAPTER 3

Data Types and Variables in Detail

In Chapter 2, you learned basic concepts like naming conventions for variables, mathematical operations, getting help, and clearing the command prompt. You also saw an overview of global variables.

In this chapter, you will explore the concepts of data types and variables in detail. The following is the list of the topics you will learn and demonstrate:

Data Types in GNU Octave

Let's create a new Jupyter notebook file for GNU Octave. You will save all the demonstrations for this chapter in this notebook.

Convert the first cell to markdown, as you did in Chapter 2, and type in and run the following code to create a heading and a sub-heading:

```
# Data Types
## Basics
```

After this, create a simple variable as follows:

```
x = 10
```

© Ashwin Pajankar and Sharvani Chandu 2020
A. Pajankar and S. Chandu, *GNU Octave by Example*,
https://doi.org/10.1007/978-1-4842-6086-9_3

You know that all variables in the current scope can be seen by the command who and you can learn the details of the variables with the command whos, as shown in Figure 3-1.

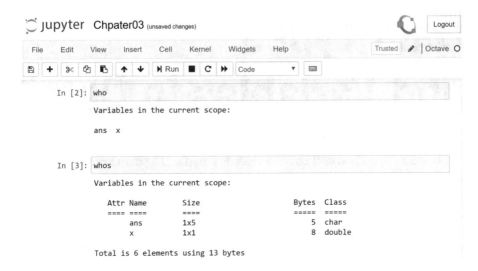

Figure 3-1. *Output of the commands who and whos*

If you notice in Figure 3-1, all of the variables are matrices by default and all of the numeric variables are double by default (you'll look at doubles a little later in this section). However, the type double requires a lot of memory. There are four signed integer types of data: int8, int16, int32, and int64. They require 1, 2, 4, and 8 bytes, respectively. Similarly, uint8, uint16, uint32, and uint64 are unsigned integer data types and they also require 1, 2, 4, and 8 bytes, respectively. You can create a variable with the desired data type as follows:

```
# Create a variable with the desired data type
y = uint8(23)
```

In this code, the code comment starts with #. Whenever the GNU Octave interpreter encounters #, it treats it as a code comment and ignores the text after it on that line. The output after running the code above and the command whos is shown in Figure 3-2.

```
In [6]: # Create a variable with the desired data type
        y = uint8(23)

        y = 23
```

```
In [7]: whos
        Variables in the current scope:

        Attr Name            Size                Bytes  Class
        ==== ====            ====                =====  =====
             ans             1x5                     5  char
             x               1x1                     8  double
             y               1x1                     1  uint8

        Total is 7 elements using 14 bytes
```

Figure 3-2. *A variable of the type uint8*

As an exercise, create variables of the other integer data types discussed above.

Floating numbers are represented by double and single precision formats. The single precision occupies 4 bytes. Out of these 4 bytes (32 bits), 23 bits are used to store the fraction, 8 bits are used for the exponent, and 1 bit is used for the sign. The double precision occupies 8 bytes. Out of these eight bytes (64 bits), 52 bits are used for the fraction, 11 bits are used for the exponent, and 1 bit is used for the sign. The following is an example of the same:

```
# Single and double precision floats
a = single(3.14)
b = double(3.14)
```

Run this code and then the command whos to see the details of the variables you created.

In the last chapter, you learned that the letters i, j, I, and J are used to represent $\sqrt{(-1)}$, which is an imaginary number. Using this number, you can define complex numbers. Run the following code:

```
# defining and understanding complex numbers
z = 2 + 3I
real(z)
imag(z)
```

The first line defines a complex number. The next two lines return the real and the imaginary part of the complex number. By default, the complex number is a double. You can explicitly define a single or a double precision complex number as follows:

```
z1 = single(2 + 3I)
z2 = double(2 + 3I)
```

Run the command whos after this to see the datatype of these complex numbers.

You can also create character strings as follows:

```
s1 = "Hello World!"
```

These are the basic data types in GNU Octave. In the next section, you will learn how to work with the multidimensional data structures known as arrays.

Arrays, Vectors, and Matrices

Just like in the programming languages C and C++, you can create and use arrays in GNU Octave. An array is collection of variables of the same datatype that are stored in continuous memory locations. Arrays can have one or more dimensions. Multi-dimensional arrays are usually called matrices. Let's see examples of arrays. Convert a cell to markdown and type the following code to create a heading:

```
# Arrays and Vectors
```

Then type and execute the following code in two different cells:

```
a = [ 1, 2, 3, 4, 5 ]
size(a)
```

The output is shown in Figure 3-3. The

```
ans = 1 5
```

means that the matrix a has one row and five columns.

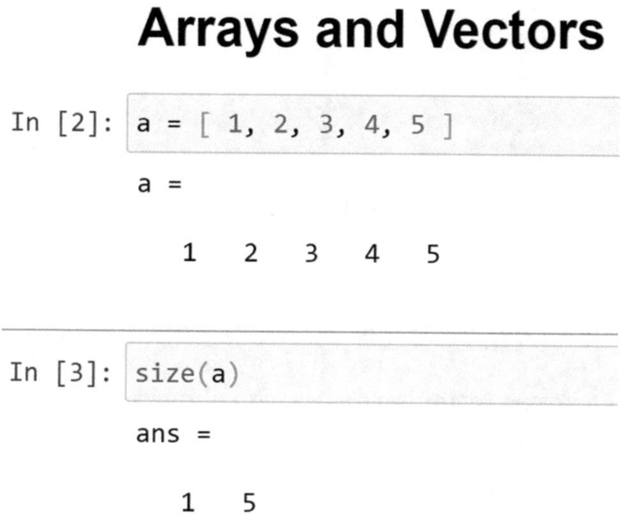

Arrays and Vectors

```
In [2]: a = [ 1, 2, 3, 4, 5 ]

        a =

            1   2   3   4   5


In [3]: size(a)

        ans =

            1   5
```

Figure 3-3. *A simple array*

You can also declare the above array as

```
a = [ 1 2 3 4 5 ]
```

The above array has only one row. You can similarly create an array with a single column as follows:

```
b = [1; 2; 3; 4; 5]
size(b)
```

The semicolon (;) is the delimiter for rows. The output is shown in Figure 3-4.

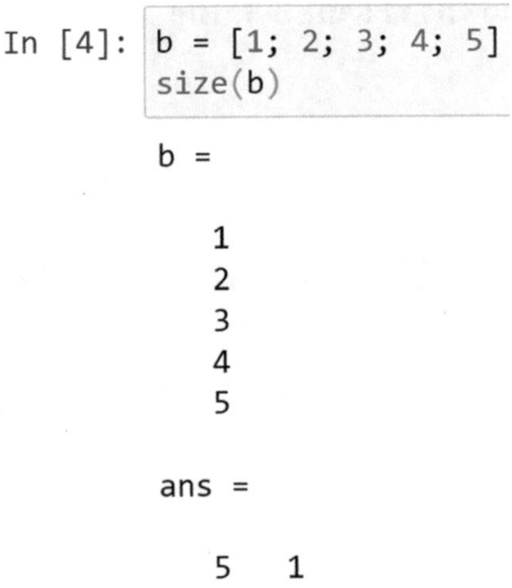

```
In [4]:  b = [1; 2; 3; 4; 5]
         size(b)

         b =

            1
            2
            3
            4
            5

         ans =

            5    1
```

Figure 3-4. *A simple array with a single column*

In GNU Octave, a vector is a matrix with either one row or one column. The above are examples of vectors.

You can even create 2D matrices as follows:

```
a = [1, 2; 3, 4]
size(a)
```

The output is shown in Figure 3-5.

```
In [5]:  a = [1, 2; 3, 4]
         size(a)
```

```
a =

    1    2
    3    4

ans =

    2    2
```

Figure 3-5. *A 2x2 2D matrix*

In the case of 2D or multi-dimensional matrices, the number of elements in every row must be equal. Otherwise the GNU Octave interpreter throws an error as follows:

```
a = [1, 2; 3, 4, 5]
error: vertical dimensions mismatch (1x2 vs 1x3)
```

If you run the command whos, you can see that the default datatype of all the arrays is double. You can create the arrays, vectors, and matrices of any custom datatype as follows:

```
a = int16([1, 2, 3])
b = int8([1; 2; 3])
c = int32([1, 2; 3, 4])
```

Indexing in Arrays

Let's use the above examples to understand indexing. Indexing starts from 1 in Octave. In C and C++, it starts from 0. So, if you have a lot of experience with C and C++ programming, be careful. You can retrieve the first element in the array a in the following ways:

```
a(1)
a(1, 1)
```

The second element can be retrieved in the following ways:

```
a(2)
a(2, 1)
```

You can retrieve the elements of a column vector as follows:

```
b(1)
b(1, 1)
b(2)
b(2, 1)
```

For the 2D matrix c, you can retrieve the elements as follows:

```
c(1, 1)
c(1, 2)
c(2, 1)
c(2, 2)
```

Operations on Arrays

You can perform mathematical operations on numerical arrays. Let's see a few operations. Create two arrays as follows:

```
a = [0, 1; 2, 3]
b = [4, 5; 6, 7]
```

Let's perform a few operations with an array as one operand and a numerical constant as the other operand:

```
a + 5
a - 3
7 - a
a * 2
a ** 2
a ^ 2
a / 2
a % 2
```

Let's perform a few operations with arrays as both operands:

```
a + b
a - b
b - a
a * b
a / b
a % b
```

Array Creation Routines

There are many array creation routines in GNU Octave. The function ones() creates a matrix of ones. The following is an example:

```
ones ( 3, 3 )
```

The function zeros() creates a matrix of zeros. The following is an example:

```
zeros ( 3, 3 )
```

The function eye() creates an identity matrix (a matrix with all of the diagonal elements as 1s and the rest as 0s). The following is an example:

```
eye ( 3, 3 )
```

The function rand() creates a matrix of random numbers. The following is an example:

```
rand ( 5, 5 )
```

Run the above examples and see the output.

Let's see two more functions and their respective output. The function linspace(base, limit, n) accepts the lower and upper limits, and creates an array with n linearly spaced elements. The following is an example:

```
linspace( 1, 10, 4 )
```

The output is as follows:

```
ans = 1    4    7    10
```

The function logspace (base, limit, n) accepts the lower and upper limits and creates an array with n logarithmically spaced elements. The following is an example:

```
logspace( 1, 5, 5 )
```

The output is as follows:

```
ans = 10    100    1000    10000    100000
```

You can assign them to variables or you can directly display their values.

As an exercise, try passing different values to these array creation functions.

Matrix Manipulation Function

Let's see a few matrix manipulation functions. Create a 2D matrix as follows:

```
a = [ 1 2 3; 4 5 6; 7 8 9 ]
```

You will use this matrix for the demonstrations of all of the matrix manipulation functions that we are going to discuss in this section. Using ' after a variable name computes the transpose of the matrix:

```
a'
```

The output is as follows:

```
1    4    7
2    5    8
3    6    9
```

You can compute the determinant of the matrix with det(a).

You can flip matrices in the various ways with the following functions:

```
flip(a)
fliplr(a)
flipud(a)
```

The function fliplr() flips the matrix left to right and the function flipud() flips up to down. You can convert a matrix into an upper and lower triangular matrix with the following functions:

```
triu(a)
tril(a)
```

Run these function calls and see the output.

Summary

In this chapter, you examined the data types in GNU Octave. You studied and demonstrated arrays and operations on them. You learned about operations on arrays and matrices. You will use many of these operations on matrices when working with images. Images are represented as multi-dimensional arrays or matrices in GNU Octave. You will also use these concepts when you study data visualization.

In the next chapter, you will explore loops, conditional statements, and functions in GNU Octave in detail.

CHAPTER 4

Loops, Functions, and Files

In Chapter 3, you learned about arrays, matrices, and vectors in GNU Octave in detail. You will use these concepts in the remaining chapters to demonstrate the functionality offered by GNU Octave.

In this chapter, you will learn concepts such as if statements, loops, functions, and file operations in detail. The following is the list of the topics you will learn and demonstrate:

- Decision making with if statements

- Loops in GNU Octave

- User-defined functions

- Global variables

- Working with files

Decision Making with If Statements

If you have worked with any programming language before, you will find this section and the next couple sections easy to comprehend. However, we don't recommend skipping anything because you must familiarize yourself with the GNU Octave syntax for the decision-making operations.

© Ashwin Pajankar and Sharvani Chandu 2020
A. Pajankar and S. Chandu, *GNU Octave by Example*,
https://doi.org/10.1007/978-1-4842-6086-9_4

The if statement is the simplest and the most basic decision-making statement. It has been around since the days of machine-language and assembly-language programming, way before modern programming languages like C and BASIC came into existence.

It's time to learn how to use the if statement for decision making. You will use a Jupyter notebook for the demonstrations in this chapter.

The following statement creates a variable named as x and assigns the value 34 to it:

```
x = 34
```

Here's the syntax of the if statement:

```
if (rem(x, 2) == 0)
    printf("Even Number!\n")
endif
```

In this statement, you are comparing the remainder of x / 2 with the number 0. If they are equal, the expression returns true and the lines in the if – endif block are executed. Otherwise, GNU Octave just skips those lines. Run this code block and see the output.

Now let's add the else block. When the condition in the if statement is not satisfied, GNU Octave runs the else block. The following is an example:

```
if (rem(x, 2) == 0)
    printf("Even Number!\n")
else
    printf("Odd Number!\n")
endif
```

The function rem() in the code snippet above computes the remainder. Note that the endif statement comes after the else block and not after the if conditions alone.

Run this code and see the output. Try assigning different values for x and run the code to see both code blocks (if and else) in action.

If you want to evaluate multiple conditions, you can use an elseif clause in the if code block as follows:

```
x=25
if (rem(x, 2) == 0)
    printf("Divisible by 2!\n")
elseif(rem(x, 3) == 0)
    printf("Divisible by 3!\n")
else
    printf("Not Divisible by 2 or 3!\n")
endif
```

First, the if statement is checked. If it returns true, then the code under the if block is executed and the rest is skipped. If the statement in the if clause returns false, then the statement in the elseif is checked. If it returns true, then it runs the code block for the elseif and rest of the code is skipped. If the statement in the elseif returns false, then the code block in the else clause is executed. Run this code. The output is as follows:

```
Not Divisible by 2 or 3!
```

You can have multiple elseif clauses in the decision-making code. GNU Octave also has a switch statement for this kind of situation, and you can find out more about it at https://octave.org/doc/v4.2.1/The-switch-Statement.html.

Loops in GNU Octave

Let's see how to create loops in GNU Octave. Before modern programming languages, loops in assembly and machine languages were written using GOTO and IF statements. However, modern programming languages like

GNU Octave provide far more sophisticated and cleaner constructs for loops. Let's see the many ways of writing loops one by one.

Let's start with the while loop in Octave. The following is an example of the while loop:

```
x = 1;
while x <= 5
    printf("x ^ 2 is %d:\n", x**2)
    x = x + 1;
endwhile
```

The while statement always checks for the condition mentioned in it at the beginning of every iteration. If the condition is true, it runs all of the following statements in order until the statement endwhile, so this code prints the squares of the integer numbers from 1 to 5 as follows:

```
x ^ 2 is 1:
x ^ 2 is 4:
x ^ 2 is 9:
x ^ 2 is 16:
x ^ 2 is 25:
```

You must make sure that the code block in the while block has statements that will render the condition false at some time if you do not want the loop to run indefinitely. You can manually terminate the loop with a break statement. Here is the same code in a slightly different style:

```
x = 1;
while 1
    printf("x ^ 2 is %d:\n", x**2)
    x = x + 1;
    if x == 6
        break
    endif
endwhile
```

We mentioned the number 1 as the condition of the while loop. It always returns true. So, the while loop runs perpetually unless you explicitly break in the code block. In the code block, an if condition that checks equality of x with 6. When it is true, the break statement is executed and the while loop ends. We programmed it in this way to demonstrate the functionality of break; it is not usually done this way.

You can write the same program with the do-until construct. The following is an example:

```
x = 1;
do
    printf("x ^ 2 is %d:\n", x**2)
    x = x + 1;
until x > 5
```

In this code, the statements between do and until are executed in each iteration until the condition in the until statement is false. As soon as the condition is true, the loop is terminated. This loop also prints the squares of the integer numbers from 1 to 5. As an exercise, try adding the break statement in the loop above.

You can also write a for loop for the same output as follows:

```
for i = 1:5
    printf("i ^ 2 is %d:\n", i**2)
endfor
```

The statements between for and endfor are executed if the loop counter denoted by variable i is between 1 to 5. In the beginning of the for loop, i is set to 1, and in every iteration, it is incremented by 1 automatically until it is 5 and then the loop is terminated. Run the program and see the output yourself. The loop by default increments by 1. If you want to increment by any other value, say 2, you modify the for statement as follows:

```
for i = 1:2:10
```

The i in this case will be 1, 3, 5, 7, 9.

This is wraps up loops in GNU Octave. In the next section, you will see how to create user-defined functions in detail.

User-Defined Functions

Functions are nothing but subroutines. If you want to use a piece of code frequently in your program, you write it as subroutine. GNU Octave offers many built-in functions and packages to perform operations. You have seen quite a lot of built-in functions already, such as rem() and printf(). Now you will learn how to write custom functions. This is very handy when you want to write your own reusable code.

The input to any function is known an argument, and the output of a function is known as a return value. Here's an example a simple function that does not accept any input (arguments) and does not return any output:

```
function []= f0 ()
    printf("Test") ;
end
```

In this code example, the words function and end are keywords. This function prints the string Test when called. f0() is the name of the function. You can call it as follows:

```
f0()
```

This will run the function and print the string. You can create a function that returns value(s) too. When the function returns only a single value, the square brackets around the return value are not needed. The following is a function that returns the value of the pi with two decimal precision:

```
function y = f1 ()
    y = 3.14;
end
```

You can call it as follows:

```
f1()
```

You can also call it as follows by assigning the returned value to a variable:

```
a = f1()
```

Now, let's see an example of a function that accepts a couple of arguments and returns a single value. We added the square brackets around the return value to demonstrate how it is written this way. As mentioned, you can write it both ways (with or without square brackets) if the function returns single value.

```
function [y] = f2 (a, b)
    y = a + b;
end
```

The function f2() accepts two arguments and returns the addition of both. You can call this as follows:

```
f2(1, 2)
```

The other way to call this is

```
m = f2(1, 2)
```

You can have a function that returns multiple values as follows:

```
function [y1, y2] = f3 (a, b)
    y1 = a + b;
    y2 = a - b;
end
```

You can call this as follows:

```
[m, n] = f3(2, 4)
```

Then you can use the values of the variable a and b separately hereafter.

Another type of function is known as an inline function. An inline function has the keyword `inline`. The interpreter replaces the function call with the function code directly in an inline function. Here's an example of an inline function:

```
f0 = inline ("sqrt(x^2+y^2)") ;
```

You can call this function as follows:

```
f0(4, 3)
```

Inline functions are good for relatively simple functions that will not be used often in the program and that can be written in a single-line expression. Inline functions can only have one expression and can only return a single variable. The returned variable can be a multidimensional matrix.

Note   Inline functions cannot access variables (including global variables) in the current session at any time.

Global Variables

Now that you have learned about functions, you can revisit the global variables from Chapter 2 to better understand their behavior.

A global variable may be accessed inside a function without passing it as a parameter. Passing a global variable to a function will make a local copy of the variable and not modify the global value.

```
global x = 0
function f(x)
    x = 1;
end
```

Notice that when you call

```
f(x)
```

it is

```
x = 1
```

But, when you print the value of x,

```
x
x = 0
```

As explained above, the local copy of the variable x is modified in the function f(x) but the global value remains the same.

Working with Files

Let's see how to work with files. You can read the data from files on the disk and store the data in files. Before you start with file-related programming demonstrations, you will learn how to run a few OS commands with a Jupyter notebook for Octave. You can even run Linux commands on the Jupyter notebook for Octave or the Octave Interactive console. This is because the GNU Octave interpreter can also interpret Linux commands. Let's see a few examples. You can see the present working directory with the following command:

```
pwd
```

The output is as follows:

```
ans = C:\Users\Ashwin\OneDrive\GNU Octave Book\First_Drafts\
Chapter04\programs
```

You can see the list of files in the current directory as follows:

```
dir
```

The output is as follows:

```
.                        .ipynb_checkpoints   test.xlsx
..                       Chapter04.ipynb
```

The files or folders that start with a . are hidden and not usually visible in the file explorer.

You can even use the Linux command ls to get the detailed output as follows:

```
Volume in drive C has no label.
Volume Serial Number is 9C4B-9156

Directory of C:\Users\Ashwin\OneDrive\GNU Octave Book\First_
Drafts\Chapter04\programs

[.]                      [.ipynb_checkpoints]
[..]                     Chapter04.ipynb
              1 File(s)              6,570 bytes
              3 Dir(s)   120,328,843,264 bytes free
```

Let's see a few file operations. First, create a matrix of size 5x5 as follows:

```
mat01 = rand (5, 5);
```

You can save this to a file as follows:

```
save file1.mat mat01
```

This command creates a file named `file1.mat` and saves it to that file. The .mat file extension is short for matrix, a data container format that is compatible with MATLAB and Octave. mat01 has values as follows:

```
 0.81598396769278381 0.92855422110525021 0.75365606653988848
0.50191794722525962 0.49488955306890497
 0.13756053717337141 0.91373377756306917 0.21944809091873169
0.86626249762210572 0.49854345466053068
 0.48677848511935479 0.90558318580210329 0.73794364985973382
0.37583995095818151 0.39386225963682803
 0.21045562411897317 0.32938941997464716 0.64352812535181725
0.69685526187959523 0.15707829430546633
 0.49126417869029831 0.21355975998368698 0.20118076472616681
0.047443232382045439 0.31718894583130069
```

Note that you are assigning random values to the matrix while creating it, so the contents of this file will be different for you. You can load this file as follows:

```
load file1.mat
```

This will load the data from the file in the variable name mentioned in the file. Since you have saved a matrix with mat01 as the variable name, you can see the same variable name after loading. You can use this statement to load and use the data in a different notebook and program too. This is one of the best ways to save your working data like matrices, arrays, and vectors. Also, you can write custom programming APIs in other high-level languages to work with this data because it is formatted data.

You can store the values of the multiple variables to a file as follows:

```
m1 = rand(2, 2); m2 = rand(3, 3); m3 = rand(4, 4);
save ( "file2.mat" , "m1", "m2", "m3" )
```

Note that this is the plaintext format and you can assign any extension of your choice to these files.

You can load the variables into memory with the usual command:

```
load file2.mat
```

You will be able to access variables m1, m2, and m3 after this command. They will have the values stored in the file for the respective variables. You can save an array into a file in binary format with the following command:

```
save -binary binfile.bin m1
```

The contents of the file are binary, so opening this file in a text editor will show you incomprehensible ASCII characters. The best way to use it is to load it into memory as follows:

```
load binfile.bin
```

You can even save the data into a CSV (comma-separated value) file format. This format is a universal file format for saving tabular data. Here's how to save it in a CSV file:

```
a = [0 1 2; 3 4 5; 6 7 8]
csvwrite('test.csv', a)
```

This will create a CSV file and save the array there. The following are the contents of the file on the disc:

```
0,1,2
3,4,5
6,7,8
```

You can load it into a variable with the following statement:

```
a1 = csvread('test.csv')
```

You can even read a CSV file hosted online into a matrix with the following command:

```
a = urlread('http://samplecsvs.s3.amazonaws.com/
Sacramentorealestatetransactions.csv')
```

If you wish to store this online file in a local file on the disc, it can be done with the following command:

```
urlwrite('http://samplecsvs.s3.amazonaws.com/
Sacramentorealestatetransactions.csv', 'local_copy.csv')
```

You can also load and save Excel files (.xlsx). For this to work, you need to download the io package from https://octave.sourceforge.io/packages.php.

Before you proceed, make sure you have the paths set correctly. In Windows, add the following two paths to your Path variable:

```
Path_to_Octave_Installation\usr\bin
Path_to_Octave_Installation\mingw64\bin
```

In Ubuntu, in the terminal before launching the Jupyter notebook, run the following command:

```
sudo apt-get install liboctave-dev
```

Now, you must install and load the io package via the following commands:

```
pkg install io.tar.gz
```

Ignore any warnings after this step.

```
pkg load io
```

Continuing with a similar example as when you experimented with CSV files, type the following commands to see for yourself how working with Excel works in Octave:

```
a = [0 1 2; 3 4 5; 6 7 8]
xlswrite('test.xlsx', a)
```

This will create an Excel file and save the array there. The following are the contents of the file on the disc:

```
0,1,2
3,4,5
6,7,8
```

You can load it into a variable with the following statement:

```
a1 = xlsread('test.xlsx')
```

This is how to work with Excel.

Summary

In this chapter, you learned how to write decision-making programs with if statements. You also learned how to write loops. You learned how to write user-defined functions and briefly explored global variables. At the end, you learned the important concept of working with various file formats like CSV and Excel.

In the next chapter, you will see how to visualize data with GNU Octave.

CHAPTER 5

Data Visualization

In Chapter 4, you learned about important programming constructs like
decision making, loops, and user-defined functions. These programming
constructs are very useful when you need to include the logic of decision
making in your program. You also learned how to work with files of various
formats and data from the Internet.

In this chapter, you will learn about data plotting and visualization
in detail. In scientific and business applications, visualization is a
very important application/step and it is often consumed by business
end-users. The following is the list of the topics that you will learn and
demonstrate in this chapter:

- Simple plots

- Plotting options

- Errorbars

- More visualizations

- 3D visualizations

After reading this chapter, you will be able to create visualizations with
GNU Octave for scientific and business applications.

© Ashwin Pajankar and Sharvani Chandu 2020
A. Pajankar and S. Chandu, *GNU Octave by Example*,
https://doi.org/10.1007/978-1-4842-6086-9_5

Simple Plots

You will use a Jupyter notebook for this chapter. It's best to create a separate, new Jupyter notebook for this chapter, as you did for earlier chapters. Now let's see how to draw simple plots. Create data points for the X and Y axes as follows:

```
x = linspace( 1, 100, 1000);
y = x + 3;
```

You use the function `linspace()` in this code to create a matrix of values in x from 1 to 1000 with a step of 100 and corresponding values for y with the equation. This will be your data, which has pairs (x, y) for points. You can draw a simple line graph as follows:

```
plot(x, y)
```

The output can be seen in the notebook itself. The output is shown in Figure 5-1.

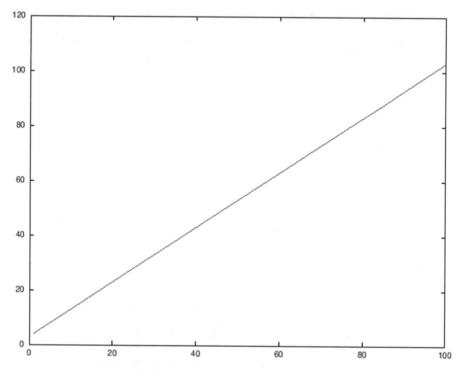

Figure 5-1. *A simple liner plot*

You can use the functionality of gnuplot to show the visualizations in different windows. Gnuplot is a command-line-driven graphics utility that works with many OSes like Windows, Linux, and Mac.

You will use the same data for the demonstration with gnuplot:

```
%plot gnuplot
plot(x, y)
```

In this code, the first line enables the gnuplot for the current session. All of the output from now on will be shown in separate windows. The output is displayed in a separate gnuplot window, as shown in Figure 5-2.

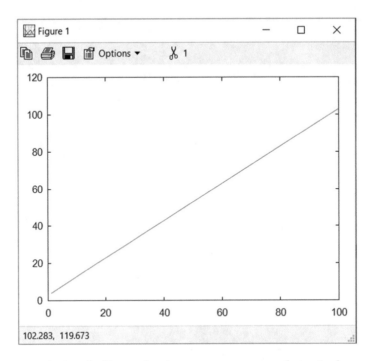

Figure 5-2. *A simple liner plot in a separate gnuplot window*

You can save your output in popular image formats as follows:

```
print("image1.png", "-dpng");
print("image2.jpg", "-djpg");
print("image3.pdf", "-dpdf");
```

You will find these images in the respective formats in the directory where you launched the Jupyter notebook server using the command prompt.

This was an example of a linear graph. Now let's plot the graph of a square function:

```
x = linspace( 1, 10, 10);
y = x.^2;
plot(x, y)
```

The output is shown in Figure 5-3.

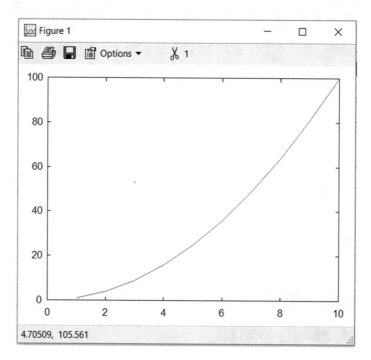

Figure 5-3. *Plot of y = x²*

You can also visualize a logarithmic graph:

```
y = log(x);
plot(x, y)
```

The output is shown in Figure 5-4.

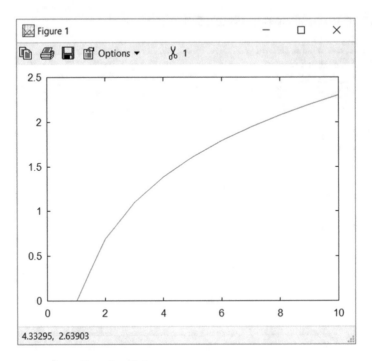

Figure 5-4. *Plot of y = log(x)*

The following is the example when data for both axes is logarithmic:

```
x = logspace( 1, 10, 10);
y = x;
plot(x, y)
```

Like linspace, logspace creates a matrix of values but with a logarithm step between the beginning and end values. The output is shown in Figure 5-5, and it is a line since both axes are logarithmic.

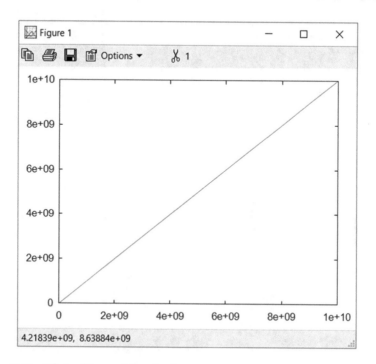

Figure 5-5. *Plot of logarithmic data*

Let's see an example of a sinusoidal:

```
x = -pi:0.01:pi;
n = 3;
y = sin(n*x);
plot(x, y)
```

In this code, you assign values from -pi to pi to the x axis with a step value of 0.01. The variable n is the number of repetitions of the sine wave. The output is shown in Figure 5-6.

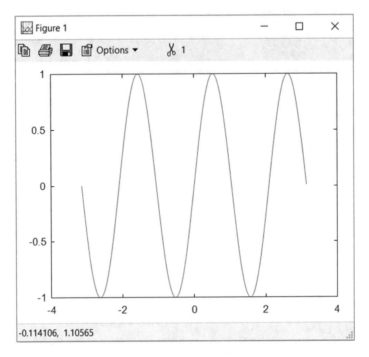

Figure 5-6. *Plot of a sine wave*

Similarly, you can plot other trigonometric functions. As an exercise, try plotting other trigonometric functions or combinations like sin(x) + cos(x).

Plotting Options

Let's see how to label axes and how to add legends. You will also add a title to the figure. Create the data first:

```
t = [0:0.01:1.0];
n = 5;
y1 = sin(2*n*pi*t);
```

Now add labels, legends, and titles as follows:

```
plot(t, y1)
xlabel('Time')
ylabel('Value')
legend('Sin')
title('Sine Plot')
```

The output has a title, a legend, and labels for the axes, as shown in Figure 5-7.

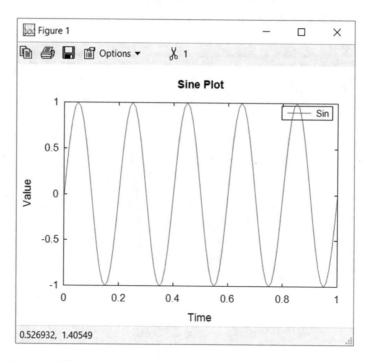

Figure 5-7. *Adding a title, legend, and labels*

You can plot multiple graphs as follows:

```
y2 = cos(2*n*pi*t);
plot(t, y1, 'r-', t, y2, 'b-.')
xlabel('Time')
```

```
ylabel('Value')
legend('Sin', 'Cos')
grid on
title('Sine and Cosine Plot')
```

As seen in the code, in plot(), you assign different styles to the graphs:
one uses a red color with a - and the other a blue color with - . -, as you
can see in Figure 5-8. You use plot() to draw multiple graphs in the same
output. Also, you turn the grid on and add a title and a legend. You use the
functions xlabel() and ylabel() to add labels to the image. You also use
legend() to identify the data in the output.

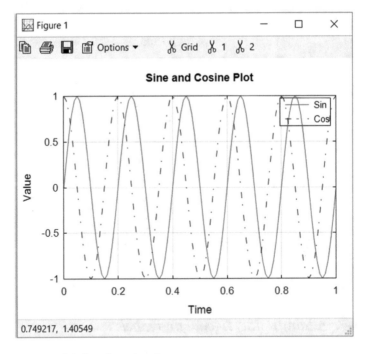

Figure 5-8. *Multiple plots in the output*

Now let's see how to use colors and styles for drawing graphs in detail. There are seven colors and seven marker styles you can use. In the plot() function call, after mentioning x and y, you must mention the color and the style. For example, k+ refers to the color black and style +. Let's see how to use all of the colors and styles. The following is the data:

```
x = [0:1:10];
y1 = x;
y2 = x + 2;
y3 = x + 4;
y4 = x + 6;
y5 = x + 8;
y6 = x + 10;
y7 = x + 12;
```

You can use marker styles and colors as follows:

```
grid on
plot(x, y1, 'k+', x, y2, 'ro', x, y3, 'g*', x, y4,
'b.', x, y5, 'mx', x, y6, 'cs', x, y7, 'wd')
```

The output is shown in Figure 5-9.

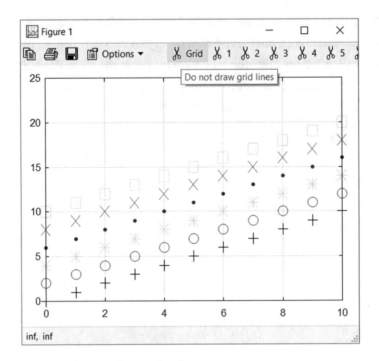

Figure 5-9. *Marker styles and colors*

You also have different line styles as follows:

```
grid on
plot(x, y1, 'k-', x, y2, 'k--', x, y3, 'k-.', x, y4, 'k:')
```

The output is shown in Figure 5-10.

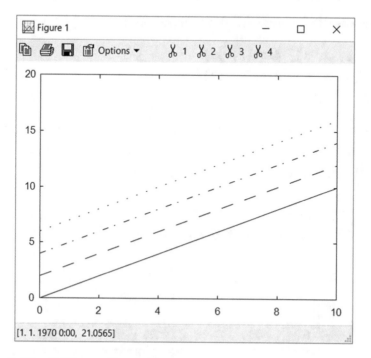

Figure 5-10. *Different line styles*

You can explore the different combinations of styles, markers, and colors yourself by changing the code snippets above.

You can also use subplots to plot multiple graphs separately in the same output window. You must use the subplot() function for this. It accepts three arguments. The first two are the dimensions of the output grid where plots are to be displayed. The last argument is the position of the plot in that grid. The following is the data:

```
x = linspace(1, 100, 100);
y1 = x.^ 2.0;
y2 = sin(x);
y3 = log(x);
```

Now use the function subplot() as follows:

```
subplot(3, 1, 1), plot(x, y1)
subplot(3, 1, 2), plot(x, y2)
subplot(3, 1, 3), plot(x, y3)
```

This code creates a grid of three rows and a column. In every row of the grid, one plot is displayed (as defined by the final argument of each subplot() call). The output is shown in Figure 5-11.

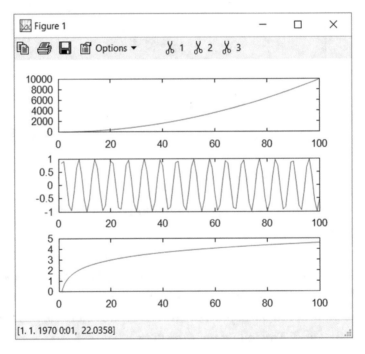

Figure 5-11. *Showing different plots with the function subplot()*

You can even show these plots in different gnuplot windows as follows:

```
close all
figure(1), plot(x, y1)
figure(2), plot(x, y2)
figure(3), plot(x, y3)
```

In this code, the statement `close all` closes and clears all of the previous visualization windows. You use the function `figure()` to create a separate window for visualization. Run the code and see the output.

Errorbars

You can even include the visualization of errors in the output. The following is a simple example:

```
close all
t = -1:0.1:1;
y = sin (pi*t);
lerr = 0.1 .* rand (size (t));
uerr = 0.1 .* rand (size (t));
errorbar (t, y, lerr, uerr);
```

In this example, you use the function `errorbar()` to visualize an error in the y-axis. The variables `lerr` and `uerr` are used to show the lower and upper value of the error for a data point. The output is shown in Figure 5-12.

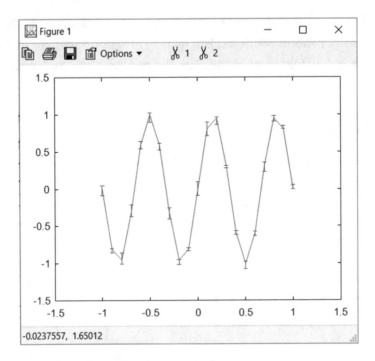

Figure 5-12. *Errorbars for the y-axis data*

Similarly, you can create errorbars for the data of the x-axis as follows:

```
errorbar (t, y, lerr, uerr, ">");
```

Note that in this code you pass an extra argument, ">", that denotes error values are for the data on the x-axis. See Figure 5-13.

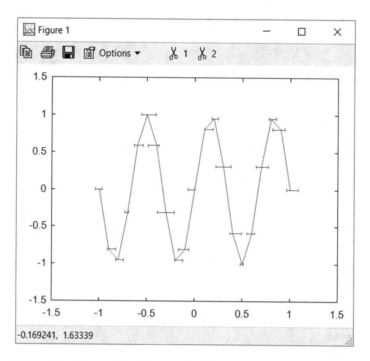

Figure 5-13. *Errorbars for the x-axis data*

Similarly, you can use "~" for error values on the y-axis. Let's see an example of how you can plot the errorbars for data for both the axes in a single visualization:

```
close all
x = 0:0.05:1;
n = 2;
err = rand (size(x))/10;
y1 = sin (n*x*pi);
y2 = cos (n*x*pi);
errorbar (x, y1, err, "~", x, y2, err, ">");
```

The output is shown in Figure 5-14.

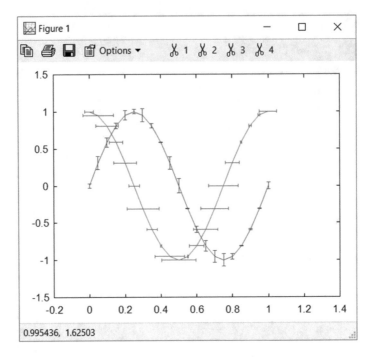

Figure 5-14. *Errorbars for the data of both the axes*

You can even create boxes in place of the errorbars with the following code:

```
errorbar (x, y1, err, err, "#r", x, y2, err, err, "#~");
```

In this function call, err stands for the error vector and r stands for the red color. You pass the same error vector for both axes. As you must have guessed, # is used to create errorboxes. It produces the output shown in Figure 5-15.

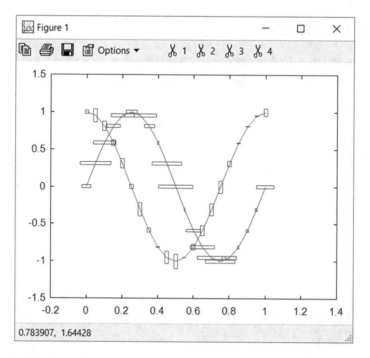

Figure 5-15. *Errorboxes*

This is how you can show the data related to the error. In all of the examples above, the data for error was simulated. But in real-life projects, you will have data from real devices as input. You can store the error margin in arrays and visualize them, as you have seen in previous examples.

More Visualizations

The graphs we have demonstrated until now use lines and curves for plotting functions. In this section, you will see how to use other types of visualizations to represent the data.

Scatter Graphs

Scatter graphs use discrete points rather than continuous curves to represent data. The following is an example of the use of function scatter():

```
close all
x = linspace(1, 100, 100);
y1 = x.^ 2.0;
grid on
scatter(x, y1)
```

The output is shown in Figure 5-16.

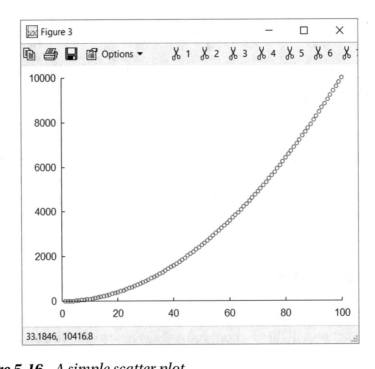

Figure 5-16. *A simple scatter plot*

You can customize the size of circles and the color as follows:

```
close all
scatter(x, y1, s = 10, filled='r')
```

The output is shown in Figure 5-17.

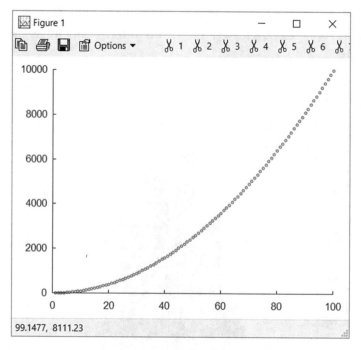

Figure 5-17. *A customized scatter plot*

Histograms

A histogram is a visual reorientation of the distribution of frequency of occurrence of elements in a dataset. In mathematics and statistics, you study frequency distribution tables. A histogram is the visualization of those tables. Write some simple code for a histogram as follows:

```
clear all
close all
a = randn(1000, 1);
hist(a)
```

In this code, you create a matrix of dimensions 1000 X 1 filled with random values from a normal distribution using the function randn(). The function hist() creates a histogram with 10 bins by default, as shown in Figure 5-18.

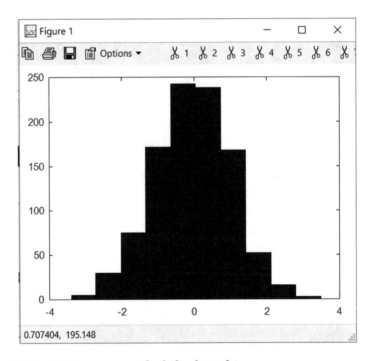

Figure 5-18. *Histogram with default 10 bins*

You can adjust the number of bins in the histogram as follows:

```
hist(a, nbins=100)
```

This code creates a histogram with 100 bins, as shown in Figure 5-19.

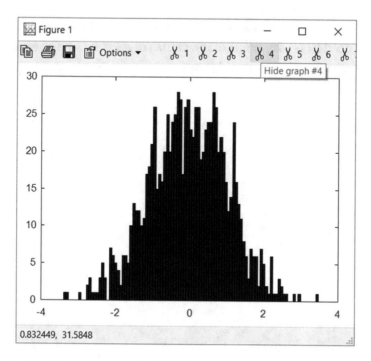

Figure 5-19. *Histogram with 100 bins*

Contours

You can represent data in the form of contours. A contour is a closed shape joining all of the points in an image that have the same value. The most prominent example of the usage of a contour is a topographic map with contour lines.

Here's an example of a contour:

```
x = [1 2 3 4 5 4 3 2 1];
y = x;
z = x' * y;
contour(z)
axis([1 9 1 9])
```

The function contour() draws contour visualizations. The function axis() is used to set the limits of the values of the axes. In the example, the limits of the x-axis are 1 to 9 and they are the same for the y-axis, as shown in Figure 5-20.

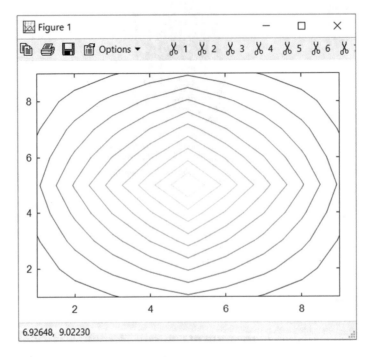

Figure 5-20. *Representation of contours*

You will revisit the concept of contour while demonstrating 3D visualizations, when you will learn and demonstrate 3D versions of contours. You will also demonstrate them with 2D contours.

Polar Graph

The polar coordinate system uses the distance from origin (r) and the angle from a fixed line (θ) to determine the position of a point in the plane. The following formula converts polar coordinates into XY coordinates:

$$x = r \times \cos(\theta)$$

$$y = r \times \sin(\theta)$$

You can draw a simple polar graph as follows:

```
theta = 0:0.1:2*pi;
rho = linspace(0.1, 0.1, 63);
polar(theta, rho)
```

The function polar() accepts values of theta and r as arguments and draws a polar graph, as shown in Figure 5-21.

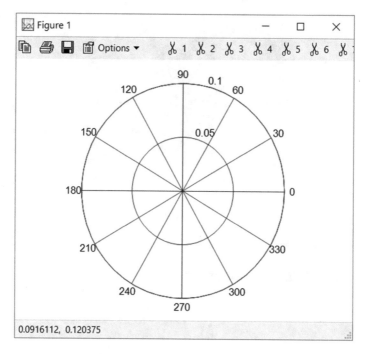

Figure 5-21. *A simple polar graph*

You can combine multiple graphs as follows:

```
theta = 0:0.02:2*pi;
rho1 = 0.4 + 1.1.^theta ;
rho2 = 3 * sin ( theta ) ;
rho3 = 5 * (1 - cos( theta )) ;
rho4 = 4 * cos (8 * theta ) ;
r = [ rho1 ; rho2 ; rho3 ; rho4 ] ;
polar ( theta , r , '.' ) ;
```

The output is shown in Figure 5-22.

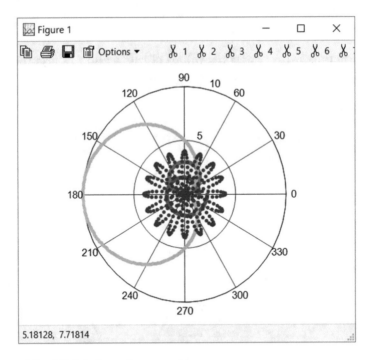

Figure 5-22. *Multiple polar graphs*

Pie Charts

You can create pie charts with Octave. These charts are mostly used in business-related visualizations. Here's how to create a simple pie chart:

```
a = [2, 3 ,5];
pie(a)
```

The function pie() divides the pie shape according to the proportion of the weight of the members of the arguments you pass to it. The output is shown in Figure 5-23.

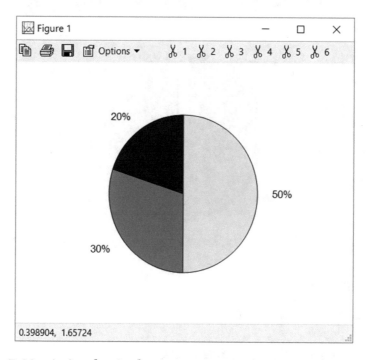

Figure 5-23. *A simple pie chart*

You can also have an exploded pie chart. You need to pass the explosion vector as the second argument to the function `pie()`:

```
e = [1, 0, 1];
pie(a, e)
```

In the explosion vector e in this code, 1 stand for enabling an explosion and 0 stands for not enabling it. The output is shown in Figure 5-24.

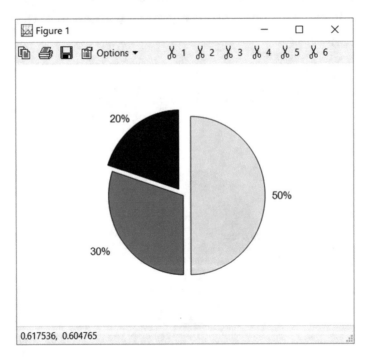

Figure 5-24. *An exploded pie chart*

Visualizing Data as Images

You can visualize your data as images using Octave. Images are represented as numbers in Octave. You will study image processing in detail in a dedicated chapter. For now, you will learn how to visualize arrays as images. You can use the function imagesc() to visualize arrays as images. Let's demonstrate this with the following code:

```
a = randn(50, 50);
imagesc(a)
```

The output is shown in Figure 5-25.

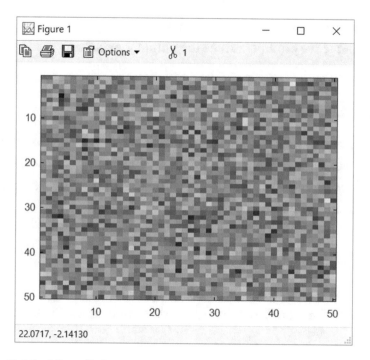

Figure 5-25. *Visualizing an array as an image*

This output is rendered with the default colormap with a jet map of 64 values. A colormap is a set of colors used to represent data. There are many colormaps supported by GNU Octave and you can find the list at https://octave.sourceforge.io/octave/function/colormap.html.

The following code visualizes the same data with another colormap:

```
imagesc(a), colorbar, colormap cool;
```

The function magic(n) returns a n×n magic square. Let's visualize it with the viridis colormap:

```
imagesc(magic(6)), colormap viridis;
```

Run both of the lines in separate cells in the Jupyter notebook or the Octave interactive prompt and see the output for yourself.

3D Visualizations

Until now, all the visualizations we demonstrated were 2D visualizations. Now you will learn and demonstrate 3D visualization. Let's use the function meshgrid(). You will use this function to create data points for a 3D visualization. Its usage is as follows:

```
y = x = [-3:1:3];
[x1, y1] = meshgrid(x, y)
```

In this code, you define the range of the variables x and y. Then you pass them to the function meshgrid(), which returns a grid of points as follows:

```
x1 =

   -3   -2   -1    0    1    2    3
   -3   -2   -1    0    1    2    3
   -3   -2   -1    0    1    2    3
   -3   -2   -1    0    1    2    3
   -3   -2   -1    0    1    2    3
   -3   -2   -1    0    1    2    3
   -3   -2   -1    0    1    2    3
```

```
y1 =

  -3  -3  -3  -3  -3  -3  -3
  -2  -2  -2  -2  -2  -2  -2
  -1  -1  -1  -1  -1  -1  -1
   0   0   0   0   0   0   0
   1   1   1   1   1   1   1
   2   2   2   2   2   2   2
   3   3   3   3   3   3   3
```

For our demonstration, you'll need a bigger grid, as follows:

```
y = x = [-10:1:10];
[x1, y1] = meshgrid(x, y)
```

Let's compute another variable, z, and then use the function mesh() to visualize (x1, y1, z) as follows:

```
z  = x1.^2 + y1.^2;
mesh(x1, y1, z)
```

The output is shown in Figure 5-26.

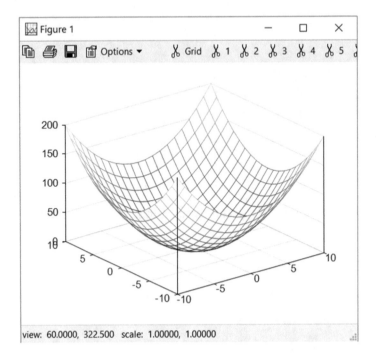

Figure 5-26. *Visualizing mesh*

As you can see, the function mesh() plots a 3D wireframe. You can change the orientation of the image by dragging it with a mouse pointer.

Similarly, the function meshc() plots mesh with underlying contour lines. Run the following function call in a new cell and see the output:

```
clf;
meshc(x1, y1, z)
```

In this code, you use the command clf to clear the earlier figure. The output of the code is shown in Figure 5-27.

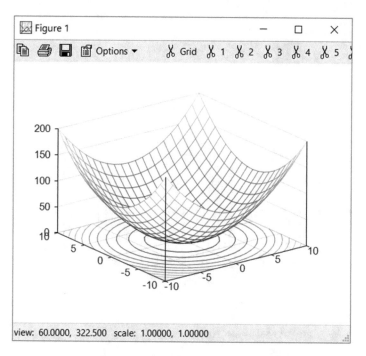

Figure 5-27. *Visualizing mesh with underlying contours*

The function meshz() draws a 3D mesh with the surrounding curtain as follows:

```
clf
meshz(x1, y1, z)
```

The output is shown in Figure 5-28.

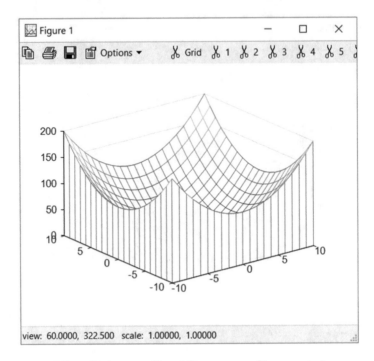

Figure 5-28. *Visualizing mesh with surrounding curtain*

Similar to wireframe mesh, there are functions to draw surfaces. The functions surf() and surface() draw surfaces using given data points. The following are examples of calls for these functions:

```
surf(x1, y1, z)
surface(x1, y1, z)
```

The output is shown in Figure 5-29.

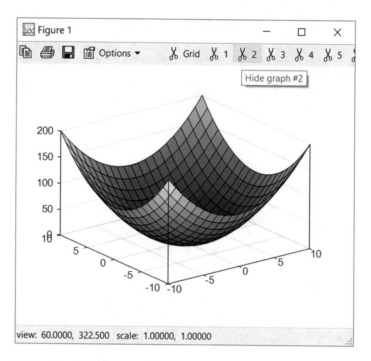

Figure 5-29. *Visualizing surface*

The function surfc() draws a surface with associated contours and surfl() draws a surface with lighting:

```
surfc(x1, y1, z)
surfl(x1, y1, z)
```

Run the above code in separate cells after the clf command and see the output.

You can even visualize 3D plots with the function plot3() as follows:

```
clf;
z = [0:0.01:3];
n = 3;
theta = n * pi * z;
plot3 (cos (theta), sin (theta), z);
```

107

The output is a spring-shaped figure, as shown in Figure 5-30.

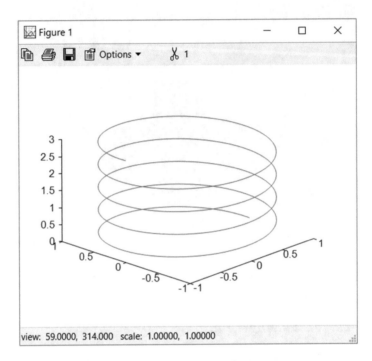

Figure 5-30. *A spring shape*

You already saw how to visualize a 2D contour, but let's revisit it before demonstrating a 3D version of a contour. The following is the data:

```
y = x = [-3:0.1:3];
[X, Y] = meshgrid(x, y);
Z = X.^3 - Y.^3;
```

A regular 2D contour looks as follows:

```
clf
contour(X, Y, Z);
```

The output is shown in Figure 5-31.

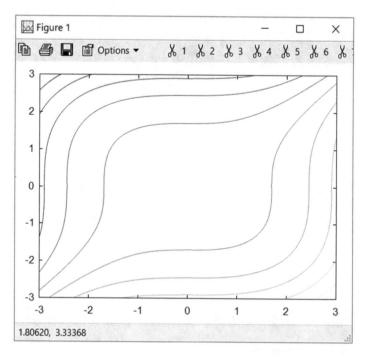

Figure 5-31. *2D contour*

You can draw a 3D contour as follows:

```
clf
contour3(X, Y, Z);
```

The output is shown in Figure 5-32.

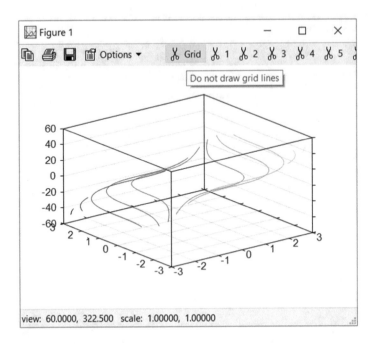

Figure 5-32. *3D contour*

As an exercise, explore the functions contourc() and contourf() with the same data.

Summary

In this chapter, you learned and demonstrated the ways to visualize multidimensional data with 2D and 3D visualizations in Octave in detail. Now you should be comfortable with the graphical representation of data for scientific and business applications, where data visualization is an important part of the data processing pipeline or architecture.

The next chapter will focus on the topic of data analytics. You will learn and demonstrate various concepts in that area in detail with GNU Octave.

CHAPTER 6

Data Analysis

In Chapter 5, you learned how to visualize data with GNU Octave. You learned how to create various types of visualizations of the data you have, such as simple plots, error bars, and 3D visualizations. Data visualization techniques are very useful in business and scientific domains.

In this chapter, you will explore assorted topics in the area of data analytics. The following is the list of topics you will learn and demonstrate in this chapter:

- Simple statistics

- Histogram

- 1-D interpolation

- 2-D interpolation

- Polynomial fitting

- Linear regression

After reading this chapter, you will be able to work in the area of data analysis using GNU Octave effectively.

© Ashwin Pajankar and Sharvani Chandu 2020
A. Pajankar and S. Chandu, *GNU Octave by Example*,
https://doi.org/10.1007/978-1-4842-6086-9_6

Simple Statistics

Create a new Jupyter notebook for this chapter, and then create a new cell as a markdown and add a heading with the following code:

```
# Simple Statistics
```

This will create a level 1 heading. Now enable GNU plotting and create a sample array as follows:

```
%plot gnuplot
x = linspace( 1, 100, 1000);
```

You can find the mean with the following code:

```
mean(x)
```

You can find the median as follows:

```
median(x)
```

You can find the mode as follows:

```
mode(x)
```

These are a few familiar statistical methods. Let's have a look at a few more methods.

You can find out the range (the difference between the maximum and minimum values in the data set) as follows:

```
range(x)
```

The interquartile range is the difference between the upper and lower quartiles of the input dataset:

```
iqr(x)
```

You can compute the mean square as follows:

```
meansq(x)
```

You can compute the standard deviation and variance as follows:

```
std(x)
var(x)
```

You can compute the skewness and kurtosis as follows:

```
skewness(x)
kurtosis(x)
```

Histogram

You can visually represent the distribution of frequency of data items. This is known as a histogram. You can use the function hist() to represent data in the form of a histogram.

The following code creates a simple histogram of data with the default number of bins (10):

```
x = rand(100, 1);
hist(x)
```

The output is shown in Figure 6-1.

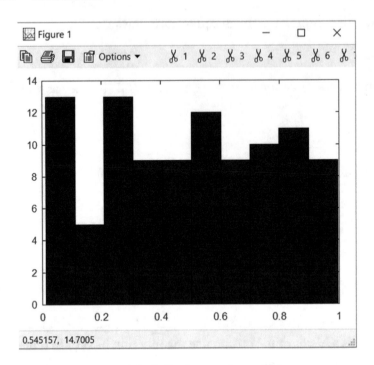

Figure 6-1. *Histogram with default number of bins*

You can plot a histogram of randomly distributed normal data with 30 bins as follows:

```
hist (randn (10000, 1), 30), xlabel('Bins'), ylabel('Count');
```

The output is shown in Figure 6-2.

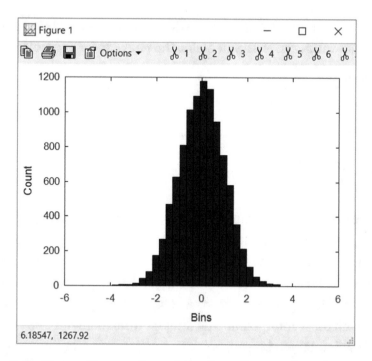

Figure 6-2. *Normally distributed random data with 30 bins*

Interpolation

Interpolation is a type of estimation technique. It is used to estimate new data points from the available data points. Suppose for function $f(x)$, you have values for the data points x=1, 2, 3, 4, and so on. Using interpolation, you can determine the values for intermediate points like x=2.5 or x=3.7. There are various types of interpolation techniques, and you will have a look at some of them in this section.

1-D Interpolation

The function interp1() returns interpolated values of a 1-dimensional function at specific points. It interpolates input data to determine the value of y_i at the points x_i. It accepts x, y, x_i, and the interpolation method

115

as arguments. The following example demonstrates the 1-D interpolation with various methods. First, you define the points to be interpolated:

```
x0 = [0:10];
y0 = cos (2*pi*x0/3);
```

You also define x1 and y1 as follows:

```
x1 = [0:0.05:10];
y1 = cos (2*pi*x1/3);
```

There are different methods to interpolate data. By default, GNU Octave does linear interpolation, where it tries to fit lines between all known data values. So "nearest" assigns the value closest to the datapoint, "pchip" is the Piecewise Cubic Hermite Interpolating Polynomial method, and "spline" interpolates by fitting a cubic spline equation. You might be familiar with these interpolation techniques from mathematics. You can read more about them for yourself.

The various interpolation methods are as follows:

```
near = interp1 (x0, y0, x1, "nearest");
lin = interp1 (x0, y0, x1);
pch = interp1 (x0, y0, x1, "pchip");
spl = interp1 (x0, y0, x1, "spline");
```

Finally, you plot everything:

```
plot (x1, y1, "r",
      x1, near, "g",
      x1, lin, "b",
      x1, pch, "c",
      x1, spl, "m",
      x0, y0, "r*"),
legend ("original", "nearest",
        "linear", "pchip",
        "spline");
```

The output is shown in Figure 6-3.

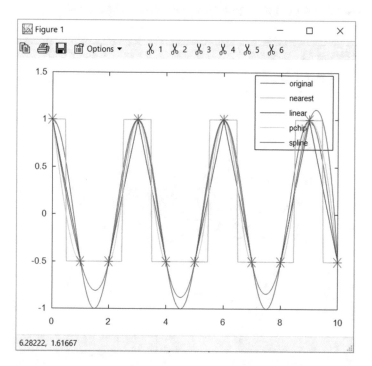

Figure 6-3. *1-D interpolation*

As you can see in Figure 6-3, the spline interpolation (represented by the dark pink color) is the one that closely resembles the expected result.

2-D Interpolation

Let's see 2-D interpolation. You will plot it with the function peak(), which is used to visualize local maxima and local minima. Let's create a surface first:

```
[X, Y] = meshgrid(-4:4);
Z = peaks(X, Y);
surf(X, Y, Z), title('Original Data');
```

In this code, you create a meshgrid to compute the peaks and then visualize the meshgrid with peaks, as shown in Figure 6-4.

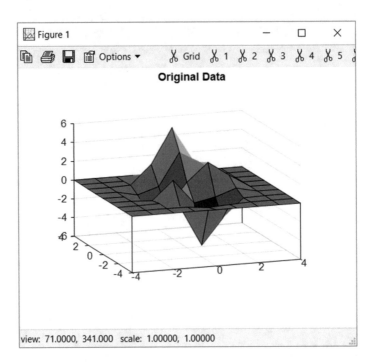

Figure 6-4. *The original data*

You can get a more detailed surface with linear interpolation. You use the function interp2() that accepts x, y, z, xp, yp, and then it computes the new value of zp. The following is the code:

```
[Xp, Yp] = meshgrid(-4:0.2:4);
Zp = interp2(X, Y, Z, Xp, Yp);
surf(Xp, Yp, Zp), title('Linear Interpolation');
```

It produces the output shown in Figure 6-5.

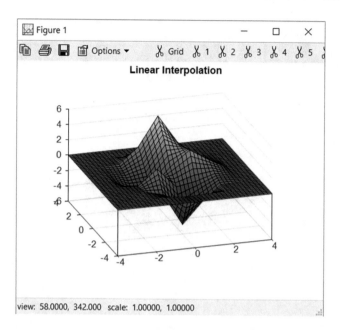

Figure 6-5. *Detailed graph with linear interpolation*

You can use the spline interpolation by adding an extra argument as follows:

```
Vp = interp2(X, Y, Z, Xp, Yp, "spline");
surf(Xp, Yp, Zp), title('Spline Interpolation');
```

The output is shown in Figure 6-6.

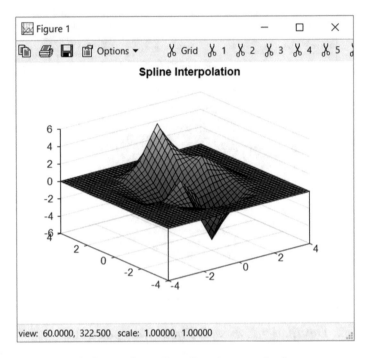

Figure 6-6. *Detailed graph with spline interpolation*

You can try the other types of methods for interpolation by passing the strings "nearest" and "pchip" as arguments.

Polynomial Fitting

You can fit a given set of points with a polynomial using the function polyfit(). You have to pass x, y, and the degree of the polynomial, and the function returns the list of coefficients for the polynomial that is the best fit for the points. Then, you use the function polyval() to evaluate the polynomial at each point. Here is the code:

```
x = linspace(0, 4*pi, 12);
y = cos(x);
```

Now, compute the list of coefficients for a ninth-degree polynomial:

```
p = polyfit(x, y, 9);
x1 = linspace(0, 4*pi);
```

Evaluate the y1 and plot it:

```
y1 = polyval(p,x1);
plot(x,y,'r*',x1,y1, 'b');
```

The output is shown in Figure 6-7.

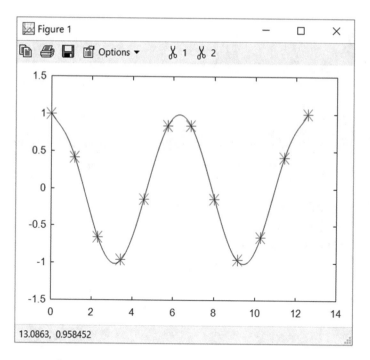

Figure 6-7. *Polynomal fitting with a curve of the ninth degree*

You can have linear regression with the degree of fitted polynomials as 1. Create the data points first:

```
x = 1:100;
y = -0.2*x + 2*randn(1, 100);
```

Now, fit the points with the polynomial of degree 1 (which is a line):

```
p = polyfit(x, y, 1);
f = polyval(p, x);
```

Now, plot it:

```
plot(x, y, 'b.', x, f, 'r-')
```

The output is shown in Figure 6-8.

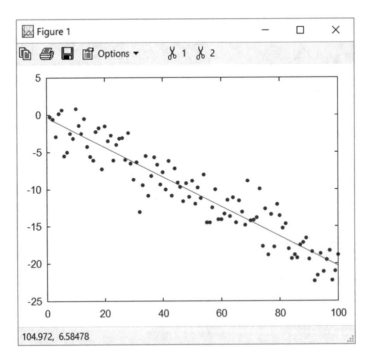

Figure 6-8. *Linear regression*

You can see from the output that this clearly is a case of linear regression; that is, you are trying to represent all the given data points with a line.

Summary

In this chapter, you learned and demonstrated simple statistical functions and histograms to represent datasets. You also explored ways to interpolate data points in one and two dimensions. You also learned polynomial interpolation and its application for linear regression. These statistical functions, histograms, and interpolation techniques are very useful in data analysis.

In the next chapter, you will explore more complex concepts and their demonstrations with GNU Octave. You will learn about signal processing in the next chapter.

CHAPTER 7

Signal Processing

In Chapter 6, you learned about data analysis in GNU Octave in detail. In this chapter, you will learn about signals, different types of signals, Fourier transform, and how to use signals in GNU Octave.

Signals

A signal, by definition, refers to a function used to convey information about a phenomenon. In electronics, you can think of signal as a voltage or current or radiation value. A signal can be of many types. It can be an audio, image, or video signal. Audio signals can be captured through a microphone. Images and videos can be captured through a camera. In the next two chapters, you will see in more detail how to work with audio, images, and videos.

Continuous and Discrete Signals

As defined above, a signal is a function. From mathematics, you know that signals can be continuous and discrete. In case of continuous signals or continuous-time signals, you can acquire the value at any arbitrary point where the signal is defined. Discrete signals are also referred to as a time series. As the name suggests, the values of the function are discrete. One of the examples of a discrete signal is a histogram, which you saw in Chapter 6. In discrete signals, you can only get the value at which the signal is defined.

© Ashwin Pajankar and Sharvani Chandu 2020
A. Pajankar and S. Chandu, *GNU Octave by Example*,
https://doi.org/10.1007/978-1-4842-6086-9_7

Let's first create a new Jupyter notebook for the exercises in this chapter. In the first cell, type the following:

```
# Signal Processing
```

Set it as markdown and then run it.

You need to install the signal processing toolbox. Do so by running the following command:

```
pkg install -forge signal
```

Load the package by running the following command:

```
pkg load signal
```

Now, let's see how to create continuous and discrete signals in GNU Octave. First, here's a continuous signal:

```
t = linspace(0, 2*pi);
x = @(t) sin(t);
```

In this code, you create a function or signal which computes values for sine between 0 and 2π. Now plot it to see what the signal looks like:

```
%plot gnuplot
figure(1), plot(t, x(t)), grid on;
```

The output is shown in Figure 7-1.

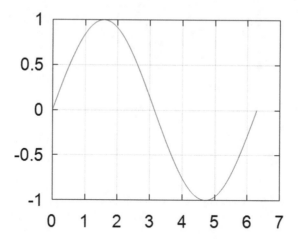

Figure 7-1. *Continuous sine signal*

You see a continuous sine signal plot.

Let's create a discrete time-series function for a sin function as follows:

```
t = [0, pi/4, pi/2, 3*pi/4, pi, 5*pi/4, 3*pi/2, 7*pi/4, 2*pi];
x = sin(t);
```

You will now plot the discrete sine signal to see how it looks:

```
%plot gnuplot
figure(2), stem(t, x), grid on;
```

The output is shown in Figure 7-2.

127

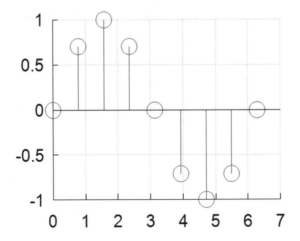

Figure 7-2. *Discrete sine signal*

You can see a sparse sine signal with a few selected points. Note that for value between 0 and 2π, you can get the value of the signal at any point in the continuous signal but for a discrete signal, you can obtain values only at the discrete values where the signal is defined. For example, you cannot get the value of x at t=2 in the discrete sine signal.

Analog and Digital Signals

An analog signal is a continuous signal; an example of an analog signal is an audio signal, which you will see in more detail in Chapter 8. These signals are smooth and you can get values with great precision, whereas a digital signal is a discrete signal that can take only a fixed number of values. A good example is the bits in a computer data stream. They can either be 0 or 1 and images, which you will see in more detail in Chapter 9. While we live in an analog world, we rely on computers for computation purposes, which is a digital world. Because of this, we tend to quantize our signals for faster computation. Quantization is the process of mapping a continuous set of values to a finite number of values.

Even and Odd Signals

If you recall functions from mathematics, every function can be expressed as a summation of even and odd signals. Even signals satisfy the following property:

```
f(-x) = f(x)
```

An example of an even signal is a cos function:

```
f(x) = cos(x)
f(-x) = cos(-x)
     = cos(x)
     = f(x)
```

And odd signals satisfy the property

```
f(-x) = -f(x)
```

An example of an odd signal is a sin function:

```
f(x) = sin(x)
f(-x) = sin(-x)
      = -sin(x)
      = -f(x)
```

In the Fourier transform section later in this chapter, you will see that a signal is a combination of sin and cos functions, which are even and odd functions. Therefore, you can use the properties of even and odd functions to form Fourier series properties. You can read more about the Fourier series and its properties by yourself.

Periodic and Non-Periodic Signals

Periodic signals are functions that repeat themselves after a fixed interval. Periodic functions satisfy the property

f(t) = f(t + T)

where T is the time period after which the signal repeats the same values.

Periodic signals can be both continuous and discrete. In addition to trigonometric functions, you can plot other period functions in GNU Octave.

Let's see how to plot a sawtooth signal:

```
t = 1:25;
sawtooth = sawtooth(t);
%plot gnuplot
figure(3), plot(t, sawtooth);
```

The sawtooth plot is shown in Figure 7-3.

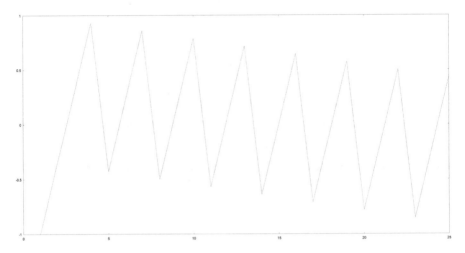

Figure 7-3. *Sawtooth signal plot*

Let's look at how to generate and plot a square signal:

```
t = 0:1/10000:1;
square = square(2*pi*5*t);
%plot gnuplot
figure(4), plot(t, square);
```

The square plot is shown in Figure 7-4.

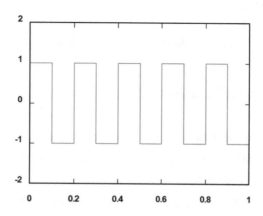

Figure 7-4. *Square signal plot*

You will now look at a few standard non-periodic signals used in signal processing. First, here's a triangular pulse:

```
t = -1:1/10:1;
triangle = tripuls(t, 0.001);
%plot gnuplot
figure(5), plot(t, triangle);
```

The triangular pulse is shown in Figure 7-5.

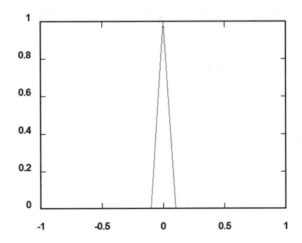

Figure 7-5. *Triangular pulse plot*

You can do the same to create a rectangular pulse or a Gaussian pulse. Note that this signal is not periodic in nature and does not satisfy the condition for periodic signals.

These are the fundamentals of some basic properties of signals and systems. You can learn more about the properties of signals by yourself.

Now let's look into a special kind of signal, the function sinc(). The mathematical equation for a sinc function is

sinc(t) = sin(t)/t

You can plot it in GNU Octave by calling the function sinc() as follows:

```
t = linspace(-5,5);
sinc = sinc(t);
%plot gnuplot
figure(6), plot(t, sinc);
```

Figure 7-6 shows the plot of the function sinc().

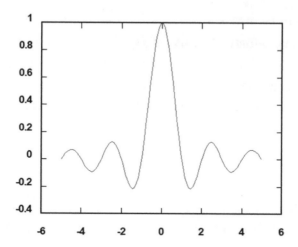

Figure 7-6. *Sinc function*

The Fourier transform of a unit pulse function is a sinc function. If you notice carefully, the sinc function takes value 1 when x is 0 and takes the value 0 for integer multiples of π.

In the next section, you will learn about the Fourier transform and how to compute a Fourier transform using GNU Octave.

Fourier Transform

In the previous section, you looked at functions that are a function of time. If you recollect from physics, time and frequency are the inverse of each other:

t = 1/f

A Fourier transform comes from the Fourier series. It is a way of expressing the function as a summation of a bunch of sinusoidal functions. The Fourier transform function is defined as follows:

$$\hat{f}(\xi) = \int_{-\infty}^{\infty} f(x)e^{-2\pi ix\xi} dx$$

A Fourier transform has a lot of applications, not just differential equations in mathematics but also in signal processing and Linear Time-Invariant (LTI) systems. As discussed, computers work with discrete values and the input signal is converted to discrete values. The Fourier transform for discrete signal is called a Discrete Fourier Transform (DFT), which is defined as follows:

$$X_k = \sum_{n=0}^{N-1} x_n \cdot e^{-\frac{i2\pi}{N}kn}$$

As this forms the basic operation of many signal processing systems, you want the transform operation to be fast. Hence, the Fast Fourier Transform (FFT) is used and is available in the signal processing toolbox. This is a fast way of computing DFT.

Here's how to compute FFT on a 1D signal:

```
t = 0:1/1000:2-(1/1000);
sin_fn = 10*sin(2*pi*10*t);
t2 = length(sin_fn);
t2 = 2^nextpow2(t2);
sin_ft = fft(sin_fn, t2);
%plot gnuplot
figure(7),
subplot(2, 1, 1), plot(t, sin_fn);
subplot(2, 1, 2), plot(abs(sin_ft));
```

In this code, you compute a Fourier transform of a sine function using FFT. The Fourier transform computed has real and complex values, hence you will plot the absolute of the FFT. The result is shown in Figure 7-7.

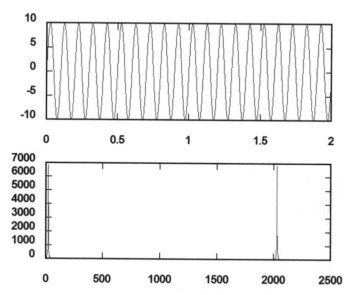

Figure 7-7. *A Fourier transform of a sine signal*

Notice the prominent peak around 2000. This corresponds to the frequency of the sine signal. Unlike the time domain signal, its Fourier transform is very sparse, which makes certain computation in the frequency domain (Fourier transform of the time signal) much faster.

Now, you will add two sin functions, one with higher frequency and the other with lower frequency:

```
t = 0:1/1000:2-(1/1000);
sin_fn1 = 10*sin(2*pi*10*t);
sin_fn2 = 10*sin(2*pi*30*t);
sin_fn = sin_fn1+sin_fn2;
t2 = length(sin_fn);
t2 = 2^nextpow2(t2);
sin_ft = fft(sin_fn);
%plot gnuplot
figure(8),
subplot(2, 1, 1), plot(t, sin_fn);
subplot(2, 1, 2), plot(abs(sin_ft));
```

The result is shown in Figure 7-8.

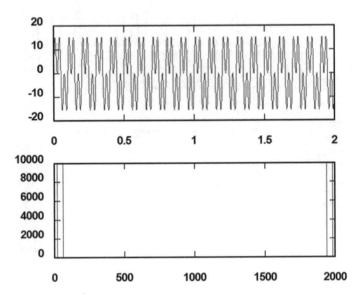

Figure 7-8. *A Fourier transform of the summation of two sine signals*

You see two peaks corresponding to the two different frequencies of the two different sine signals.

Note If you have heard of low-pass filtering, in the frequency domain, the frequency peaks pertaining to the high frequency are removed, which essentially smoothens the signal in the time domain.

You can construct the original signal from a Fourier transformed signal. In other words, to convert the signal from the frequency domain to the time domain, you can use ifft. You can explore the inverse Fourier transform function in GNU Octave by yourself.

Note We will discuss FFT in the 2D domain in Chapter 9.

If you have heard about convolution operations, a Fourier transform simplifies the computation of a convolution operation by a multiplication of the Fourier transform of the functions. This is a very interesting operation and with the growing demand for deep learning, these fundamentals are important. You can learn more about this by yourself.

Summary

In this chapter, you learned about signals, various types of signals, and the Fourier transform.

In the next chapter, you will look at audio processing in GNU Octave.

CHAPTER 8

Audio Processing

In Chapter 7, you learned about processing signals with GNU Octave. Audio is a type of signal and its processing requires detailed knowledge of signal processing. So, as a continuation of the previous chapter, in this chapter you will learn how to process audio with GNU Octave. The following is the list of topics that you will explore in this chapter:

- Reading an audio file
- Creating your own audio file
- Plotting the sound wave signal

By the end of this chapter, you will be able to work with audio files and process audio signals.

Reading an Audio File

Create a new Jupyter notebook for this chapter. We have recorded an audio file named `sample.wav`. As you can see, it is in WAV (Waveform Audio File Format). You can use other file formats like OGG or MP3 too. Create a string for the filename as follows:

```
file = 'sample.wav'
```

© Ashwin Pajankar and Sharvani Chandu 2020
A. Pajankar and S. Chandu, *GNU Octave by Example*,
https://doi.org/10.1007/978-1-4842-6086-9_8

You can retrieve information about the audio file with the function audioinfo() as follows:

```
info = audioinfo (file)
```

The output is as follows:

```
info =

  scalar structure containing the fields:

    Filename = C:\Users\Ashwin\OneDrive\GNU Octave Book\First_
    Drafts\Chapter08\programs\sample.wav
    CompressionMethod =
    NumChannels =  2
    SampleRate =  44100
    TotalSamples =  70560
    Duration =  1.6000
    BitsPerSample =  16
    BitRate = -1
    Title =
    Artist =
    Comment =
```

You can read the data stored in the audio file into GNU Octave numerical arrays with the function audioread() as follows:

```
[M, fs] = audioread(file);
```

It returns two values. Depending on the number of channels, M is a one- or two-column array. We recorded a stereo audio clip so it has two channels. You can also see the number of channels in the previous output. fs is the sampling frequency (mentioned as sample rate in the previous output). It is 44100 Hz in this case, which is one of the standard values in the domain of audio. It is usually used by digital audio CDs. The other standard frequency is 48 kHz (48000 Hz).

The function audioread() has many parameters. You can use it as follows to read the file in the native datatype of the stored audio:

```
[M, Fs] = audioread(file, datatypes = 'native');
```

You can also specify the datatype in which you want to read the audio file:

```
[M, Fs] = audioread(file, datatypes = 'uint8');
```

Creating Your Own Audio File

You can create your own signals and write them as an audio file. You have to use function audiowrite() for this. The following is an example:

```
filename='sine.wav';
fs=44100;
t=0:1/fs:10;
w=2*pi*440*t;
signal=sin(w);
audiowrite(filename, signal, fs);
```

The example creates a sine wave and you can even play it using an audio player. The duration of the wave is 10 seconds. You can play it with a built-in audio player in GNU Octave using the functions audioplayer() and play(), as follows:

```
[M, fs]=audioread(filename);
player=audioplayer(M, fs, 8);
play(player)
```

Plotting the Sound Wave Signal

Let's see how to use the function plot() to plot the audio wave signal.
Create two small audio signals of 0.01 seconds for this, as follows:

```
signal1='signal1.ogg';
signal2='signal2.ogg';
fs=44100;
t=0:1/fs:0.01;
w1=2*pi*440*t;
w2=2*pi*660*t;
audiowrite(signal1,sin(w1),fs);
audiowrite(signal2,sin(w2),fs);
```

The signals have different frequencies. You visualize the first signal,
signal1, as follows:

```
%plot gnuplot
[M1, fs] = audioread(signal1);
plot(M1)
```

The output is shown in Figure 8-1.

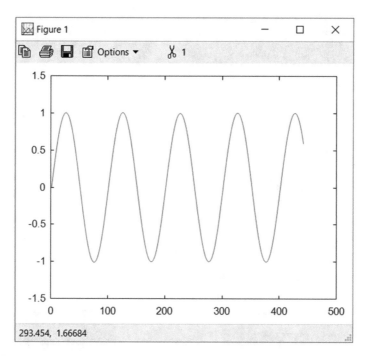

Figure 8-1. *Sine wave*

You can add two signals and visualize as follows:

```
[M2, fs] = audioread(signal2);
plot(M1+M2)
```

The output is shown in Figure 8-2.

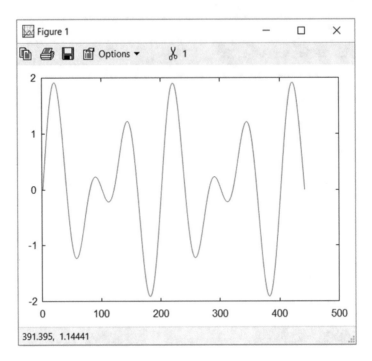

Figure 8-2. *Two added sine waves*

You can multiply two sinusoidal functions as follows:

```
audiowrite('product.wav', M1.*M2, fs);
[M3, fs]=audioread('product.wav');
plot(M3);
```

The output is shown in Figure 8-3.

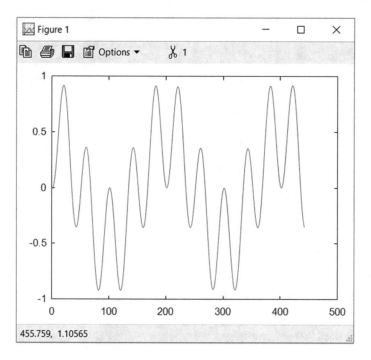

Figure 8-3. *Two sine waves multiplied*

You can divide two signals as follows:

```
audiowrite('div.wav', M1./M2, fs);
[M4, fs]=audioread('div.wav');
plot(M4);
```

The output is shown in Figure 8-4.

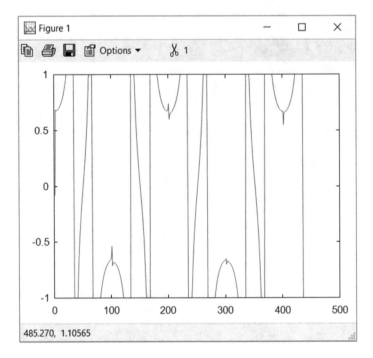

Figure 8-4. *Division of sine waves*

This is how you work with audio signals.

Summary

In this chapter, you learned and demonstrated how to process audio signals. You also saw how to read and write audio signals. You have seen how to perform mathematical operations on audio signals. As discussed, audio processing is a form of signal processing and these techniques are very useful in the domain of audio processing.

The next chapter teaches you more complex applications of signal processing with GNU Octave. You will learn about image and video processing in detail in the next chapter.

CHAPTER 9

Image and Video Processing

In Chapter 8, you learned about audio processing in GNU Octave in detail. In this chapter, you will use some of the concepts you learned about in Chapter 7 to understand image processing.

In this chapter, you will learn about the following list of topics:

- Image processing

- Video processing

Image Processing

With the growing availability of good cameras in phones over the past few years, and the outbreak of social media platforms like Instagram, YouTube, etc. users all over the world can now upload visually pleasing images and videos. All photo editing applications, like **Photoshop** or **GIMP**, used for this purpose employ image processing. In this section, you will learn how to process digital images with GNU Octave.

You will first look at the basic installation required to work with images and then move on to writing your own code to work with them.

Similar to previous chapters, you must install the image package available at https://octave.sourceforge.io/image/index.html.

© Ashwin Pajankar and Sharvani Chandu 2020
A. Pajankar and S. Chandu, *GNU Octave by Example*,
https://doi.org/10.1007/978-1-4842-6086-9_9

You will use a Jupyter notebook for all of the demonstrations in this chapter. Create a new notebook for this chapter. In a new cell in the Jupyter notebook, run the following command:

```
pkg install -forge image
```

Next, load the image package by running the following command:

```
pkg load image
```

Let's first explore how to read and write images. For this, download any image from the web or use any image on your computer, and save it in the current folder of your Jupyter notebook with the name **sample_color. jpg**. We will use the image in Figure 9-1 to demonstrate the results in this chapter.

Figure 9-1. *A sample image*

Loading, Displaying, and Resizing Images

Now you'll learn how to load the images into Octave. Type the following command into a new cell in the notebook:

```
color_image = imread('sample_color.jpg');
```

imread loads the image and stores it to a variable, in this case color_ image. Now display the image:

```
%plot gnuplot
figure(1), imshow(color_image);
```

This will display the image in a new window. If you zoom into the image, you will notice the image looks like small squares, as you can see in Figure 9-2.

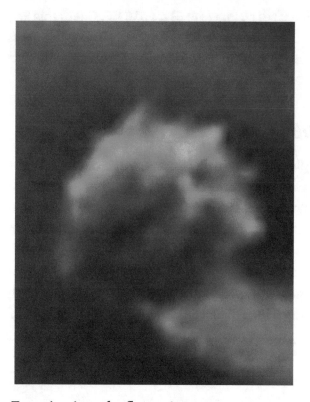

Figure 9-2. *Zooming into the flower image*

149

The reason you see the small squares in the image is because the image is stored as three-dimensional matrix and each member is an 8-bit unsigned integer (uint8).

Let's get the size of the image:

```
size(color_image)
```

You will see something like this in the output:

```
ans = 3648 5472 3
```

In this case, the image is a matrix of dimensions 3648 X 5472 X 3. You can resize the image using `imresize`:

```
resized_image = imresize(color_image, [512, 512]);
```

Here you resize the image to 512 X 512 X 3. Check this for yourself using `size`. When using `imresize()`, you can either give a scale to which you want to resize the dimensions or directly mention the size to which you want to resize, as you have done here.

Color Space

Now let's explore how the data is stored and how the image obtains its color. You have seen that the size of an image has three dimensions and the third dimension has the value 3. This is true for all color images. Each 2D matrix of the third dimension is called a channel. The first is for red (R), the second is for green (G), and the third is for blue (B). You must be familiar with the acronym RGB; this comes from the channel names.

A color space is a specific way of organizing colors such that they can be reproducible in digital representation. With a triplet of each value corresponding to the intensity in R, G, and B colors, you can cover most of the colors that the human eye can perceive.

Now let's explore the concept visually. In a new cell, type the following code:

```
red_image = color_image;
red_image(:,:,2) = 0;
red_image(:,:,3) = 0;

%plot gnuplot
figure(2), imshow(red_image);
```

In this code, you copy the color_image to red_image and then set the green and blue channel values to 0. The image is shown in Figure 9-3. Only the red component of the image is visible in the image. You can try for yourself for the other two channels or with a combination of two channels.

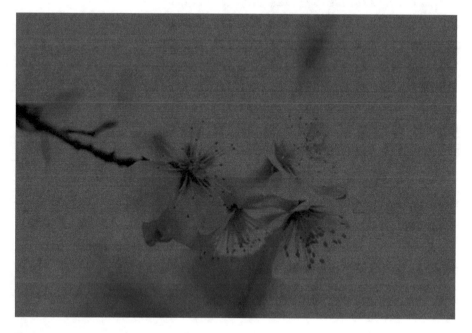

Figure 9-3. *Red channel of the flower image*

You are all familiar with old pictures or movies that are monochromatic. So, if having only one channel is displaying the image in that color space, then how do you get monochromatic images? Before we jump into that, let's look at the data stored in the image. For that, let's display the values in a small portion of the image like this:

```
color_image(1:10, 1:10, 2)
```

You will see something like this in the Jupyter notebook (not the exact same values, because they will depend on your image):

```
ans =130 125 125 125 124 124 126 126 124 123 121
127 126 125 124 121 123 125 124 123 126 124
126 126 125 126 123 123 124 124 124 124 123
126 127 127 128 126 125 123 124 125 123 122
126 127 126 127 126 126 123 123 123 122 121
125 123 123 124 126 126 124 122 121 122 121
125 124 123 123 125 125 123 121 121 123 121
125 125 125 125 124 123 122 122 121 125 122
125 127 126 126 123 122 121 124 122 124 122
123 129 127 125 124 122 123 124 122 120 120
124 124 124 125 125 123 124 124 124 124 123
```

Note that the values are between 0-255. This is because the image is stored with an uint8 datatype and it has range of 0-255 ($2^8=256$), as discussed.

To get a monochromatic image, the three channels are combined to one. You usually do this using the following function:

```
gray_image = rgb2gray(color_image);
```

```
%plot gnuplot
figure(3), imshow(gray_image);
```

The output is shown in Figure 9-4.

Figure 9-4. *Gray scale image of the flower*

You can see the display of the monochromatic image. This is also called a grayscale image.

Now let's see the size of the gray_image:

```
size(gray_image)
ans = 3648 5472
```

You will notice that the size of the gray_image is the same as the size of the color_image, except for the three color channels.

There are other color spaces, which you can explore by yourself. Some of the important ones are RGB and HSV (Hue-Saturation-Value).

Cropping, Rotating, and Saving Images

You are all familiar with basic photo viewing or editing tools that lets us crop or flip images. In this section, you will explore these cool features and then learn how to save an image.

Let's first look at cropping. In a new cell, run the following code:

```
crop_image = color_image(2000:3000, 2000:4000, :);

%plot gnuplot
figure(4), imshow(crop_image);
```

Make sure that you do not exceed the limits of the image size you are using.

The output is shown in Figure 9-5.

Figure 9-5. *The cropped image*

In this way, you can crop out the portion you want in your own images if you know the desired pixel location.

Let's now look at flipping and rotating images:

```
up_down_flip_image = flipud(color_image);

%plot gnuplot
figure(5), imshow(up_down_flip_image);
```

This code flips the image along the horizontal, as shown in Figure 9-6.

Figure 9-6. *Horizontally flipped image*

Similarly, you can also flip the image along the vertical axis, as shown in Figure 9-7:

```
left_right_flip_image = fliplr(color_image);

%plot gnuplot
figure(6), imshow(left_right_flip_image);
```

Figure 9-7. *Vertically flipped image*

You can also do a flip both horizontally and vertically like this:

```
flip_image = fliplr(flipud(color_image));

%plot gnuplot
figure(7), imshow(flip_image);
```

You can do the same using `imrotate()`, like this:

```
rotated_image = imrotate(color_image, 180);

%plot gnuplot
figure(8), imshow(rotated_image);
```

Here, you rotated the image by 180 degrees to get the same image as shown in Figure 9-8 as the previous code. You can try for yourself with different angles in `imrotate()`.

Figure 9-8. *Vertically and horizontally flipped image or image rotated by 180 degrees*

If you want to save any of the images you modified, you can do so using imwrite:

```
imwrite(rotated_image, 'flipped_image.jpg');
```

The first parameter to the function is the image you want to save and the second one is the string with the path to the image you want to save along with the image name.

FFT2

In Chapter 7, we discussed FFT (Fast Fourier Transform). In this section, you will look at the Fourier transform for images. In images, frequency corresponds to how fast the pixel intensity changes. When there are fast changes, it is a high frequency region; if little changes, it is a low frequency region. The applications of the concepts you study here form the basics of low-pass filtering/smoothing and high-pass filtering/edge detection, which are the fundamentals of many advanced image processing techniques. You can explore more on your own once you are clear on the fundamentals.

FFT2 computes a discrete Fourier transform on the 2D matrix. For this, first create a 2D pulse image:

```
pulse_2d = zeros(500, 500, 3);
pulse_2d(246:255, 246:255, :) = 255;
pulse_2d = im2bw(pulse_2d);
```

This will generate a 2D pulse image as shown in Figure 9-9.

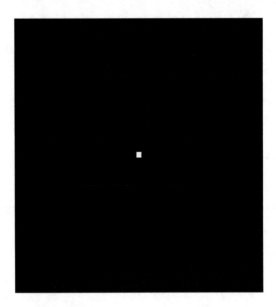

Figure 9-9. *2D pulse*

Let's now compute the Fourier transform on this image:

```
pulse_freq = fft2(pulse_2d);
```

Before displaying the image, you need to first get the absolute value of the frequency and then do any fftshit to align the center to the center of the image. Recall that this is similar to the function `sinc()`, which you saw in a previous chapter, extended to 2D, where the peaks of the sinc function are white with a maximum value and the valleys of the sinc function are black with a minimum value, as shown in Figure 9-10.

Figure 9-10. *Fourier transform of 2D pulse*

Video Processing

In this section, you will explore the basic workings of video processing. Normally, videos are conceptually visualized as a 4D object, the fourth dimension being time. Imagine it to be something like Figure 9-11.

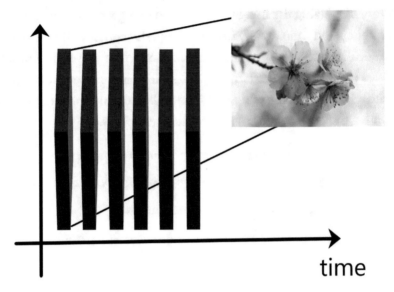

Figure 9-11. *Visual interpretation of videos*

First, to work with videos, you need to install the video package. Follow the steps similar to what you did to install the image package:

```
pkg install -forge video
pkg load video
```

Now generate a video and write it to a video file:

```
w = VideoWriter("images.mp4");
open(w);
for i = 1:360
    img = imrotate(color_image, i);
    img = imresize(img, [512, 512]);
    writeVideo(w, img);
endfor
close(w);
```

In this code, you first create a video writer and then you open the file.

For your learning purposes, you are utilizing functions you learned in the previous sections of this chapter.

You use a `for` loop to rotate the image and resize it. And then you write each frame into the video file. Resizing images is important because all of the image frames in a video should be of the same dimensions, as shown in Figure 9-11. You can use any video format that is supported by Octave; this demonstration uses the **.mp4** format.

Here's how to read the video file:

```
w = VideoReader ("images.mp4");
while (!isempty(img = readFrame(x)))
    imshow(img);
endwhile
```

This code reads each frame from the video file and then displays it using `imshow`. You can explore more advanced techniques using what you learned in this section.

Summary

In this chapter, you learned how to read, save, and display images. You also learned about color spaces of images, plus cropping, flipping, and rotating images. You looked at a Fourier transform on images. You also learned how to read and write videos.

The next part is the Appendix. It covers several small topics that could not find place in the previous chapters.

Appendix

You have explored the functionalities offered by GNU Octave in detail. In this Appendix, you will explore assorted topics that are not covered in the earlier chapters because they do not fit in the overall narratives of those chapters. However, these functionalities are extremely useful for beginners as well as experienced programmers.

Structures

A structure is a data type that can be used to group items of the same and/or different types. If you have worked with the C programming language, you must have programmed with structures. A structure is a very versatile data type that can be used in scientific programming. Let's create a structure for such calculations. Create a new Jupyter notebook for Octave and type in the following code in the first cell to create a heading:

```
# Structures
```

Convert the cell to a markdown type and run it to create a nice H1 heading.

You can create a structure for storing information about planets as follows:

```
planet.name = 'Earth'
```

© Ashwin Pajankar and Sharvani Chandu 2020
A. Pajankar and S. Chandu, *GNU Octave by Example*,
https://doi.org/10.1007/978-1-4842-6086-9

Run the above code in a new cell and it will create a new structure with an attribute. The name of the structure is `planet` and the attribute is `name`. Now add more attributes to this structure:

```
planet.mass = 5.972 * 10^24
planet.type = 'Rocky'
```

This will add two more attributes to the structure. You can see the attributes individually by running the following code:

```
planet.name
planet.mass
planet.type
```

You can check all of the attributes with a single line of code as follows:

```
planet
```

You can define the structure with all of the attributes in a single line of code as follows:

```
planet1 = struct("mass", 1.898 * 10^27,
"name", 'Jupiter',
"type", 'Gas Giant');
```

Cell Arrays

You can store different data types under a single variable with another type of variable known as a cell array. A cell array is a container-like structure that stores strings and numerical values. Here's how you create a cell array for the example you saw earlier:

```
planet1 = {1.898 * 10^27, 'Jupiter', 'Gas Giant'}
```

This creates a cell array. You can see all of the members with the following line:

```
planet1
```

You can also access the members individually with indices as follows:

```
planet1{1}
planet1{2}
planet1{3}
```

Operations for Structures and Cell Arrays

Let's see a few operations on attributes of structures and members of cell arrays. You will demonstrate this with matrix multiplications. So define a structure with two matrices:

```
mat1 = struct("a", [1 2; 3 4], "b", [1; 2]);
```

You can perform operations on the attributes of the structure as follows:

```
mat1.a * mat1.b
```

The output is as follows:

```
ans =

    5
   11
```

You can define an equivalent cell structure:

```
mat2 = {[1 2; 3 4], [1;2]};
```

The same operation will be as follows:

```
mat2{1} * mat2{2}
```

The output will be exactly the same.

Polynomials in Octave

GNU Octave can handle polynomials in a special way. Suppose you have a polynomial as follows:

$$f(x) = 5x^2 + s + 2$$

You can represent this polynomial with a vector of coefficients as follows:

```
p1 = [5 3 2]
```

It can be evaluated for a certain value for x (in this example x=0) as follows:

```
polyval(p1, 0)
The output is as follows:

ans = 2
This is how you work with polynomials in GNU Octave.
```

Convex Hull

The convex hull, or convex closure or convex envelope, for a set of points is defined as the smallest convex polygon such that all of the points are in or on it. GNU Octave has the function convhull() to compute the convex hull for a set of points. Create a pair of x and y coordinates for a set of points as follows:

```
%plot gnuplot
clf
x = [-5 : 0.02 : 5];
y = cos(x);
```

The convex hull for the pair of x and y coordinates can be computed as follows:

```
k = convhull (x, y);
```

Let's plot it now. The points in the set are represented by green dots and the hull is represented by the red line:

```
plot (x, y, 'g.', x(k), y(k), 'r-');
axis ([-5.5, 5.2, -1.2, 1.2]);
```

The output is shown in Figure A-1.

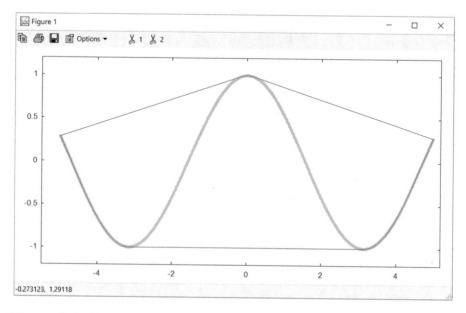

Figure A-1. *Demonstration of the convex set*

Index

A

Analog signal, *see* Continuous/continuous-time signals

Analytics
histogram, 113–115
interpolation (*see* Interpolation method)
learning goals, 111
statistics, 112–113

Arrays
command creation, 53
indexing, 54
matrix, 51
multi-dimensional array, 50–51
operations, 54–55
routines creation, 55–56
single column, 52
2D matrix, 52–53

audioinfo() function, 140

Audio processing
audioplayer()/play() functions, 141
learning goals, 139
reading audio file, 139–141
sound wave signal
divide signals, 145–146
plot()function, 142
sine waves, 143–144
sinusoidal functions, 144–145
audiowrite() function, 141

B

BODMAS/PEDMAS, 35, 36

C

Cell array, 164–165
Command line interface (CLI), 19
Continuous/continuous-time signals, 125–128
Contours, 95–96
Convex hull/closure/envelope, 166–167

D

Data types
command results, 48
complex numbers, 50
floating numbers, 49
heading and sub-heading, 47
numeric variables, 48–49

© Ashwin Pajankar and Sharvani Chandu 2020
A. Pajankar and S. Chandu, *GNU Octave by Example*,
https://doi.org/10.1007/978-1-4842-6086-9

Printed in the United States
By Bookmasters